THE DIARY OF ONE NOW DEAD

THE DIARY OF ONE NOW DEAD

TOM DRODGE

THE CRASH OF THE *TIME'S A WASTIN'* IN SAGLEK, LABRADOR

FLANKER PRESS LIMITED
ST. JOHN'S

Library and Archives Canada Cataloguing in Publication

Drodge, Tom, 1949-, author
The diary of one now dead / Tom Drodge.

Issued in print and electronic formats.
ISBN 978-1-77117-560-9 (softcover).--ISBN 978-1-77117-572-2 (EPUB).--
ISBN 978-1-77117-630-9 (Kindle).--ISBN 978-1-77117-631-6 (PDF)

    1. Hodge, Grover Cleveland--Diaries. 2. Bomber pilots--United
States--Diaries. 3. A-26 Invader (Bomber). 4. Airplane crash survival--
Newfoundland and Labrador--Labrador. I. Title.

TL553.7.D76 2018   613.6'9   C2017-907527-6
                                               C2017-907528-4 .

© 2018 by Tom Drodge

PRINTED IN CANADA

MIX
Paper from
responsible sources
FSC® C016245

This paper has been certified to meet the environmental and social standards of the Forest Stewardship Council® (FSC®) and comes from responsibly managed forests, and verified recycled sources.

Cover Design by Graham Blair

FLANKER PRESS LTD.
PO BOX 2522, STATION C
ST. JOHN'S, NL
CANADA

TELEPHONE: (709) 739-4477   FAX: (709) 739-4420   TOLL-FREE: 1-866-739-4420
WWW.FLANKERPRESS.COM

9 8 7 6 5 4 3 2 1

We acknowledge the financial support of the Government of Canada through the Canada Book Fund (CBF) and the Government of Newfoundland and Labrador, Department of Tourism, Culture, Industry and Innovation for our publishing activities. We acknowledge the support of the Canada Council for the Arts, which last year invested $157 million to bring the arts to Canadians throughout the country. *Nous remercions le Conseil des arts du Canada de son soutien. L'an dernier, le Conseil a investi 157 millions de dollars pour mettre de l'art dans la vie des Canadiennes et des Canadiens de tout le pays.*

Preface

To begin a story such as this, one must do it justice. This story is so moving and touching and so real, it is as if you are there in the plane with these men.

I have done quite a bit of research regarding this story, but because of the time between then and now, most of the people who would have remembered this plane have since moved on.

I have tried to tap into the few who I have been able to contact, but time wasn't on my side. Finding relatives of the deceased seemed almost impossible, but I had some success, and within the pages that lie ahead, I have narrated some of their testimonies as they recalled them.

This book is one of courage and endurance. Without divine intervention, these men would not have survived as long as they did.

The saddest part of this story is that, had they all lived a little longer, they would have been saved. It appears that no search party was ever begun to look for the downed plane. Had there been, the outcome of this story would have been quite different.

As you read this story, I know that you will find yourself experiencing the emotions of those men who so bravely and fiercely fought for their lives, expecting each moment that someone would locate them.

The setting for this story is during the peak of World War II. Many countries were at war with each other, and the Germans were out with their subs all along the coast of the Atlantic Ocean to try and stop the Western Allies from sending aid to Britain. At that time, Labrador was a part of the Dominion of Newfoundland. Newfoundland and Labrador became a Canadian province in 1949. The Americans had set up base in Greenland in 1942 and also in the province of Newfoundland and Labrador. This province played a strategic role in the war. The Atlantic Ocean was a war zone with little chance of escape for those who sailed its waters. It was dangerous, to say the least, for those who participated in the war, both in the air and on the water.

One of the fiercest battles ever fought was the Battle of the Atlantic, as history records. But for those who have never heard of it, the following provides some background.

THE DIARY OF ONE NOW DEAD

1
Battle of the Atlantic

Many reading this book may have some connection to the Battle of the Atlantic. Many young men had gone to war in those days to help fight for their country. For some it was a job, but others, who were old enough and in good health, were conscripted. In other words, they were forced to go and fight for their country or else go to prison. At the bottom of the Atlantic Ocean are thousands of young men who had never made it home to see their families again.

If you ever fly over the Atlantic Ocean and look out through the windows of the plane, say a prayer and thank the Lord that it was their sacrifice that gave us our freedom we have today. We will never know what could have become of those young men had they had a chance to live out the rest of their lives. As long as men live, there will always be war in some form or another. Whether it is just to keep the peace or for territorial boundaries, wars will never cease. Where we live today is nothing more than a battleground, yet it was meant to be peaceful.

The Battle of the Atlantic was the longest continuous military campaign in WWII. It ran from 1939 to the surrender and defeat of the Germans in 1945. The height of the war was from the mid-1940s through the end of 1943.

Germany had its U-boats, other warships, and aircraft, and it used them against the Royal Canadian Navy, the Royal Navy, and Allied merchant shipping vessels. There were convoys, mostly from North America and mainly going to the United Kingdom. The Soviet Union was protected for the most part by the British and Canadian armies and air force. These forces were aided by ships and aircraft from the US from September 13, 1944, onward. Italian submarines joined the German submarines after Italy entered the war on June 10, 1940.

German U-Boat

The United Kingdom, an island nation, depended on imported goods, and Britain required more than a million tons of imported material per week in order to be able to survive and fight. This was the situation the Brits found themselves in. Britain was struggling to survive as the Germans and their allies desperately tried to stop the flow of merchant shipping and war supplies from reaching its shores. Their aim was to prevent the buildup of Allied supplies and equipment in the British Isles in preparation for the invasion of occupied Europe. It seemed the only way to push back the Germans would be a defeat of the U-boat threat. Winston Churchill stated that "the Battle of the Atlantic was the dominating factor all through the war. Never for one moment could we forget that everything happening elsewhere on land, at sea, or in the air depended ultimately on its outcome."

The outcome of the battle was a strategic victory for the Allies. The German blockade was stymied, but at a great cost: 3,500 merchant ships and 175 warships were sunk and 783 U-boats were lost.

The name "Battle of the Atlantic" was coined by Winston Churchill in February 1941. It was one of the longest and most complex naval battles in history. This war lasted six years and involved thousands of ships in more than 100 convoy battles and perhaps 1,000 single-ship encounters covering thousands of square miles of ocean. The ocean was the battleground, and the advantage constantly changed in favour from one side to the other, as each gained the upper hand when new equipment was developed.

The Allies gradually gained the high ground, overcoming German surface raiders by the end of 1942 and defeating the U-boats by mid-1943. This didn't stop the U-boats, though, which continued operating until the war was over.

It was on March 1, 1941, that the Lord of the Admiralty, A. V. Alexander, asked Parliament for more ships and a great number of men to fight the Battle of the Atlantic.

In the First World War, submarine usage by the Germans was unrestricted. It would appear that they had an advantage over ships, and it was difficult for anyone to spot them. In fact, some countries wanted submarines banned. What did materialize was that the submarines were to abide by certain rules. Also, if they came across a ship, they were required to give crews plenty of time to escape and see to the safety of their men.

In 1939, when WWII was declared, the Germans had several warships at sea, and these ships immediately attacked British and French shipping. Even though the Nazis lacked the right to challenge the British Royal and French Navies, they were willing to give it their best shot. Within hours of the beginning of the war, the German *U-30* struck and sank the liner SS *Athenia*, in breach of its orders not to sink passenger ships.

At the outbreak of the war, the British and the French immediately began to blockade the Germans, although it had little effect upon them. They tried a different strategy, allowing for the protection of trade. Convoys from the Royal Navy were to concentrate their efforts near the one place the U-boats were guaranteed to be found. Some British naval officers, particularly Winston Churchill, sought out a more offensive strategy.

The Royal Navy formed anti-submarine hunting groups based on aircraft carriers to patrol the shipping lanes in the western approaches. It didn't work that well, because the submarines were usually able to detect ships as well as aircraft before the Allies had a chance to find them.

The U-boats weren't as successful as they intended; it appeared that when they shot at their targets, the torpedoes would explode prematurely, or hit and fail to explode, or run beneath the target without exploding. Not a single British warship was sunk by a U-boat in more than twenty attacks. First blame was placed on the crew, until finally the problem was diagnosed.

There was a difference in the magnetic fields at high altitudes and a slow leakage of high-pressure air from the submarine into the torpedoes' depth-regulation gear. The problems were overcome by March 1941, and the submarine ruled the waters again.

The Germans believed that the only way they could bring Britain to her knees would be through effective submarine warfare, because Britain depended mainly on overseas commerce. Their system was called the "wolf pack." In this strategy, U-boats spread out in a long line across the projected course of a convoy. When they sighted a target, they would come together and attack. Escorting warships would chase the individual submarine, and the rest of the pack would be able to attack the merchant ships with impunity.

Vice Admiral Karl Dönitz, commander of the German U-boats from 1935 through 1943, calculated that if they could knock out 300 of the latest "Atlantic boats," it would be enough to weaken the ships that traversed the Atlantic with merchandise and would starve Britain out of the war. This was different than the traditional way of doing things, whereby the submarine was used as a lone ambusher waiting outside an enemy port to attack ships entering and leaving. This tactic was used by the British submarines in the Baltic during WWI, but it wasn't successful when port approaches were well protected.

The Germans occupied Norway, and France in the spring of 1940. Italy entered the war in June, which transformed the war at sea. As a result, Britain lost her biggest ally, the French Navy, which was the fourth-largest in the world. Because of this, the Royal Navy had to stretch itself a lot farther. This also meant that Britain had to reinforce her Mediterranean fleet and establish a new group at Gibraltar to replace the French fleet in the western Mediterranean.

The U-boats gained direct access to the Atlantic by now having German bases in France. Close proximity to the Atlantic enabled them to attack convoys farther west to spend more hours on patrol, and doubling the effective size of their U-boat force. Because of the increased patrolling of the U-boats, the British destroyers were directed to leave the Atlantic. The Royal Navy fleet was taking a beating, and many older destroyers were withdrawn from convoy routes. By the summer of 1940, Britain was facing a serious threat of invasion. Many destroyers were kept busy in the channel, and they suffered heavy losses under the assaults.

Britain was now helpless, except for the large merchant fleets they had acquired in Norway and the Netherlands, which came under British control. After the Germans occupied Denmark and Norway, Britain occupied Iceland and the Faroe Islands, planting its foothold there and preventing a German takeover.

The U-boats celebrated a string of victories from June 1940 to February 1941. It was labelled their heyday. They were most successful from June to October 1940 when more than 270 Allied ships were sunk. This period of time was considered the "happy time" by the U-boats' crews. Winston Churchill would write sometime later, "the only thing that ever frightened me during the war was the U-boat period."

The biggest challenge for the U-boats was to find the convoys in the vastness of the ocean. Even though the Germans had a handful of long-range aircraft, the primary means of sighting a convoy was the U-boat itself.

Despite the success of the U-boats, they were still not recognized as the primary threat to the North Atlantic convoys. Surface warships were the ultimate commerce destroyers.

The Germans continued to fight and sink ships. The British were forced to provide battleship escorts to as many convoys as possible. This helped save convoys from the slaughter by the German battleships. The Germans were relentless.

In May of 1941, the Germans mounted the most ambitious raid of all. It was called "Operation Rheinubung." A new battleship called the *Bismarck*, and the cruiser *Prinzeugen*, were put to sea to attack convoys. The British fleet interrupted the raiders off Iceland.

In the battle of the Denmark strait, the battle warship HMS *Hood* was blown up and sunk, but the *Bismarck* was damaged and had to head to France for repairs. En route it was disabled by an air strike and sank three days later. This marked the end of the warship raids.

2
HMS *Hood*

The following lyrics, written by Johnny Horton, sum up the battle between the *Bismarck* and the HMS *Hood*:

"SINK THE *BISMARCK*"

by Johnny Horton and Tillman Franks

In May of 1941 the war had just begun
The Germans had the biggest ship
that had the biggest guns
The *Bismarck* was the fastest ship that ever sailed the sea
On her decks were guns as big as steers and shells as
big as trees

Out of the cold and foggy night came the
British ship the *Hood*

And every British seaman, he knew and understood
They had to sink the *Bismarck*, the terror of the sea
Stop those guns as big as steers and those shells
as big as trees

We'll find the German battleship that's makin' such a fuss
We gotta sink the *Bismarck* 'cause the
world depends on us
Yeah hit the decks a-runnin' boys and
spin those guns around
And when we find the *Bismarck* we gotta cut her down

The *Hood* found the *Bismarck* and on that fatal day
The *Bismarck* started firing fifteen miles away
"We gotta sink the *Bismarck*" was the battle sound
But when the smoke had cleared away the
mighty *Hood* went down

For six long days and weary nights they
tried to find her trail
Churchill told the people put every ship asail
'Cause somewhere on that ocean I know she's gotta be
We gotta sink the *Bismarck* to the bottom of the sea

The fog was gone the seventh day and
they saw the morning sun
Ten hours away from homeland the
Bismarck made its run

The Admiral of the British fleet said,
"Turn those bows around"
We found that German battleship and
we're gonna cut her down

The British guns were aimed and
the shells were coming fast
The first shell hit the *Bismarck*,
they knew she couldn't last
That mighty German battleship is just a memory
"Sink the *Bismarck*" was the battle cry that
shook the seven seas

We found the German battleship,
'twas makin' such a fuss
We had to sink the *Bismarck* 'cause
the world depends on us
We hit the deck a-runnin' and
we spun those guns around
Yeah we found the mighty *Bismarck*
and then we cut her down

In February 1942, the Germans sent some of their ships back to Germany, which ended the threat in the Atlantic. The loss of the *Bismarck* and Arctic convoys, and the perceived invasion threat to Norway, persuaded Hitler to withdraw.

The Germans had big plans, but they were a little too

late. Their U-boat losses and aircraft had suffered catastrophic losses.

German battleship *Bismarck*

HMS *Hood*

3

Battle Intensifies

After this, the British decided that they had to increase their presence in the North Atlantic crossing.

To do so, they decided to establish a base for their escort forces in St. John's, Newfoundland and Labrador. This way they could escort their convoys from Canadian ports to Newfoundland, and then on to a meeting point south of Iceland, where the British escort groups would take over. They accomplished this by sailing six Canadian destroyers, seventeen corvettes reinforced by seven destroyers, and three sloops and five corvettes of the Royal Navy. Up until 1941, the United States remained neutral; only now they were finding themselves becoming more and more involved.

President Roosevelt extended the Pan-American security zone east almost as far as Iceland. Meanwhile, the British forces occupied Iceland when Denmark fell to the

Germans in 1940. The United States was persuaded to provide forces to relieve British troops on the island.

By 1941 the United States realized that the Atlantic had become dangerous for unescorted American as well as British ships. After the sinking of the SS *Robin Moor*, the US made a decision to either recall its ships from the ocean or enforce its right to the free use of the seas.

SS *Robin Moor*

Aircraft ranges were constantly improving, but the Atlantic was far too large to be covered completely. A plan was put in place to mount ramps on some of the cargo ships and equip the vessels with a lone expandable hurricane fighter aircraft. When a German bomber plane approached, the fighter was boosted off the end of the ramp with a large rocket, to shoot down or scare off the German aircraft.

As the war raged on and technology began to improve,

one of the more important developments was directional-finding radio equipment. The wolf pack relied heavily on this same technology to easily locate the convoys. With it, the British could easily keep track of the U-boats. This was a key factor in helping them suppress and sink many of the German submarines.

One tactic that seemed to work against the German U-boats, introduced by Captain John Walker, was the "hold down," where a group of ships would patrol over a submerged U-boat until it ran out of air and was forced to surface.

For the next couple of years, it was a battle for dominance. The Germans were having pretty good success in the sinking of British ships, but they lost a few U-boats as well.

The climax of the war came in the spring of 1943. The Germans had so many U-boats on patrol in the North Atlantic that it was difficult for the convoys to evade detection.

It appeared the Germans were winning the war. It was so bad that the British considered abandoning the convoy entirely. But then the tide changed. For two months the British destroyed quite a few U-boats and took significantly fewer losses themselves. Now the wolf packs no longer had the advantage: their losses began to take their toll.

The turning point was the battle that centred on the slow convoy ON5, April–May 1943. It involved forty-three merchantmen escorted by sixteen warships. The convoy was attacked by no less than thirty U-boats. Although thirteen merchant ships were lost, six U-boats were sunk by the convoy. The merchantmen utilized the protection of land-based air cover, which culminated in Grand Admiral Karl Dönitz calling off the attack. A couple of weeks later, five or more U-boats were destroyed, with no losses to the British. Faced with disaster, Dönitz called off operations in the North Atlantic, saying, "We have lost the Battle of the Atlantic." The month of May 1943 was remembered as "Black May" by the Germans.

In that month, forty-three U-boats had been destroyed, thirty-four of them in the Atlantic. This counted for twenty-five per cent of the U-boats' total operational strength. In the same time period the British lost fifty-eight ships, thirty-four of them in the Atlantic.

In essence, the Battle of the Atlantic was won by the Allies in two months. The single biggest reason was the sudden convergence of technologies combined with an increase in Allied resources. During the final two years of the war, the Germans made several attempts to upgrade their U-boat force. They improved their anti-aircraft defences, radar detectors, torpedoes, decoys, and snorkels, the latter allowing U-boats to run underwater off their diesel engines. However, despite all these new improvements, they saw fewer victories and more losses for their U-boats. After four months of battle and heavy losses, the Germans decided to call off the offensives. Even though they never stopped trying, none of their measures were truly effective, and by 1943 the Allied air power was so strong, U-boats were being attacked in the Bay of Biscay shortly after leaving port.

The Germans had lost the technologies race. Many U-boats were destroyed over the next two years. With the battle won by the Allies, supplies poured into Britain and North Africa for the liberation of Europe.

The Germans fought to the end. In the first week of May 1945, twenty-three U-boats were sunk in battle while attempting to flee to Norway. The last actions of the Battle of the Atlantic took place on the May 7–8.

In May 1945, *U-320* was the last U-boat sunk in action. The Allied minesweeper *NYMS 382* and the freighters *Sneland* and *Aumdale Park* were torpedoed in separate incidents just hours before the Germans surrendered. The remaining U-boats at sea or in port were surrendered to the Allies, 174 in total. Most were destroyed in Operation Deadlight after the war.

4

Outcome of the Battle

The Germans failed to stop the strategic flow of supplies to Britain which helped build up troops and munitions needed for the D-Day landing.

It is maintained by some historians that the U-boat arm came close to winning the Battle of the Atlantic. The Allies were almost defeated and Britain was brought to the brink of starvation. Historian Alan Levin states that this is a misperception and that it is doubtful they ever came close to achieving this, and a sober assessment confirms his view.

First, the Battle of the Atlantic was not a contest for naval supremacy but a sustained attack on Allied commerce, which cannot by itself win command of the sea.

Second, the focus on U-boat successes, the "aces" and their scores, the convoys attacked and the ships sunk, served to camouflage the Kriegsmarine's manifold failures.

Third, unlike the Allies, the Germans were never able to mount a comprehensive blockade of Britain, nor were they able to focus their effort by targeting the most valuable cargoes: the eastbound traffic carrying war *matériel*. The reason for this misperception may be found in the postwar writings by authors Clay Blair, Jr. and Daniel Francois Jeroen van der Vat.

Clay Blair, an American historian best known for his books on military history, attributes the distortion to propagandists who glorified and exaggerated the successes of German submarines. He believes Allied writers had their own reasons for exaggerating the peril. Blair concludes "at no time did the German U-boat force ever come close to winning the Battle of the Atlantic or bringing on the collapse of Great Britain."

Daniel Francois Jeroen van der Vat, a journalist, writer, and military historian with a focus on naval history, suggests that, unlike the US, Canada, Britain, and other dominions which were protected by oceanic distances, Britain was at the end of the transatlantic supply route closest to German bases; for Britain it was a lifeline.

It is that which led Winston Churchill's concerns, coupled with a series of major convoy battles in the space of a month. It undermined confidence in the convoy system in March 1943 to the point Britain considered abandoning it, not realizing the U-boats had already effectively been defeated. These were "over-pessimistic threat assessments," according to van der Vat.

The following is a table of Allied shipping losses in the Battle of the Atlantic during World War II. All shipping losses are in gross registered tons (GRT).

Month	Year	Imports To Allies	Sunk By U-boats	Sunk By Aircraft	Sunk By Warship Or Raider	Sunk By Mines	Total Allied Shipping Sunk	German U-Boats Lost
Sep.	'39	3297070	153879	0	5051	29537	158930	2
Oct.	'39	3576135	134807	0	32058	29490	166865	5
Nov.	'39	4408689	51589	0	1722	120958	53311	1
Dec.	'39	4466664	80881	2949	22506	82712	106336	1
Jan.	'40	4847044	11263	23693	0	77116	134956	1
Feb.	'40	4348820	169566	853	1761	54740	172180	6
Mar.	'40	4970525	62781	8694	0	35051	71475	1
Apr.	'40	5336917	32467	13409	5358	19799	51083	5
May	'40	5362873	55580	158348	6893	47716	220127	1
Jun.	'40	284113	105193	61857	86087			0
Jul.	'40	195825	70193	80796	33598			2
Aug.	'40	267618	53283	63350	11433			3
Sep.	'40	295335	56328	96288	8269			1
Oct.	'40	352407	8752	32134	32548			1
Nov.	'40	146613	66438	123671	46672			2
Dec.	'40	212590	14890	55728	54331			0
Jan.	'41	2651399	126782	8597	80796	17107	302601	0
Feb.	'41	2621795	196783	89305	89096	16507	372205	0
Mar.	'41	2864121	243020	113314	138906	23585	474879	5
Apr.	'41	2620531	249375	323454	91579	24888	616469	2
May	'41	3466204	325492	146302	15002	23194	486796	1
Jun.	'41	3594684	310143	61414	7759	15326	389316	4
Jul.	'41	3765724	94209	9275	5792	8583	109276	0
Aug.	'41	4002450	80310	23862	24897	1400	125550	4
Sep.	'41	267134	202820	40812	22910	14948	259866	2
Oct.	'41	4203224	156554	35222	3305	19737	191776	2
Nov.	'41	3336789	62196	23015	17715	1714	85211	5
Dec.	'41	3735419	124070	72850	6661	63853	203581	10
Jan.	'42	327357	57086	3275	10079			3

Month	Year	Imports To Allies	Sunk By U-boats	Sunk By Aircraft	Sunk By Warship Or Raider	Sunk By Mines	Total Allied Shipping Sunk	German U-Boats Lost
Feb.	'42	476451	133746	0	7242			2
Mar.	'42	537980	55706	25614	16862			6
Apr.	'42	431664	82924	131188	15002			3
May.	'42	607247	59041	19363	18795			4
Jun.	'42	700235	54769	48474	19936			3
Jul.	'42	476065	74313	54358	8905			11
Aug.	'42	544410	60532	50516	0			9
Sep.	'42	485413	57526	24388	0			10
Oct.	'42	619417	5686	7576	5157			16
Nov.	'42	729160	53868	19178	992			13
Dec.	'42	330816	4853	12312	1618			4
Jan.	'43	203128	25503	7040	18475			6
Feb.	'43	359328	75	4858	34153			19
Mar.	'43	627377	65128	0	884			15
Apr.	'43	327943	3034	1742	11961			15
May.	'43	264853	20942	0	1568			41
Jun.	'43	97753	6083	17655	4334			17
Jul.	'43	242145	106005	7176	72			37
Aug.	'43	86579	14133	0	19			25
Sep.	'43	118841	22905	9977	4396			10
Oct.	'43	97407	22680	0	19774			26
Nov.	'43	66585	62452	8538	6666			19
Dec.	'43	86967	75471	0	6086			8
Jan.	'44	92278	24237	6420	7176			16
Feb.	'44	92923	21616	2085	0			20
Mar.	'44	142944	0	7840	7176			25
Apr.	'44	62149	19755	0	0			21
May.	'44	24424	2873	0	0			24
Jun.	'44	57875	9008	1812	24654			25
Jul.	'44	63351	0	7219	8114			24
Aug.	'44	98729	0	7176	7194			35
Sep.	'44	43368	0	0	1437			22
Oct.	'44	7176	0	0	4492			13
Nov.	'44	29592	7247	1141	0			8
Dec.	'44	58518	35920	0	35612			15
Jan.	'45	56988	7176	2365	16368			14
Feb.	'45	65233	7177	3899	18076			21
Mar.	'45	65077	0	3968	36064			33
Apr.	'45	72439	22822	0	8733			53
May.	'45	11439	7176	0	0			35

22

Because of its close proximity to Europe, the province of Newfoundland and Labrador became of strategic importance during WWII, when air bases were constructed at Gander, Stephenville, Goose Bay, and Argentia. Newfoundland and Labrador has had a long aviation history. It was the starting point of the earliest successful attempt at transatlantic flight, which was made by Alcock and Brown, who took off from Lester's Field in St. John's on June 14, 1919.

These bases resulted in several aircraft wrecks and shipwrecks. These sites have been issued "Borden Numbers" and are protected as archaeological sites. The aircraft wreck mentioned in this book that crashed near Saglek Bay, Labrador, is part of this province's archaeological inventory.

5

Borden Numbers

In Canada, all sites are coded by the Borden System. Borden numbers were created by Charles E. Borden at the University of British Columbia in 1954. It assigns a location with a sequence of four letters (Dc Ru) and a number (4) relating to a fixed map code.

Canada is divided into a grid of main map units of two degrees latitude by four degrees longitude. Latitudinal coordinates are assigned capital letters from A through U from south to north, and longitude is designated by capital letters A through V from east to west. Each two-by-four-degrees main unit (192 km x 300 km) is further subdivided into ten minute subunits designated by lowercase letters from south to north (latitude) and east to west (longitude). For example, in DcRu4, the first two letters indicate the site is in one of the sixteen-kilometre-wide grid squares in the latitudinal "D" square, and the last two letters likewise show the grid position on the longitude. The number 4 means it was the fourth site found within a sixteen-kilometre-by-sixteen-kilometre unit.

6

Greenland

In 1942, during the Second World War, the Americans had an air base established in the Kujalleq municipality of southern Greenland. The airfield was called Bluie West One.

In 2010, Kujalleq's population was 158. Around this municipality there is a thriving tourism whose attractions include a great diversity of wildlife, gemstones, tours to glaciers, and an airfield museum. In Greenlandic the name of the settlement means "Great Plain."

This story begins in Greenland, a country within the kingdom of Denmark, located between the Arctic and Atlantic Oceans, east of the Canadian Arctic Archipelago.

In terms of area, at 2,166,086 square kilometres, Greenland is the world's largest island.

It has been inhabited for at least 4,500–5,000 years by Arctic peoples whose forebears migrated there from Canada. The Norsemen settled on the uninhabited southern part of Greenland beginning in the tenth century, and the Inuit peoples arrived in the thirteenth century. The Norse colony disappeared in the fifteenth century.

Although it is a part of the continent of North America, Greenland has been associated with Europe and was ruled by Denmark and Norway for centuries. Greenland became a Danish colony in 1814 and a part of the Danish realm in 1953, under the constitution of Denmark. In 1979, Denmark granted home rule to Greenland, and in 2008, Greenland voted to transfer more power from the Danish royal government to the local Greenland government.

The early Scandinavian settlers gave the country its name. In Icelandic sagas, it is said that the Norwegian-born Icelandic Erik the Red had a farm west of Kujalleq, which was the principal city of Greenland at the time. He was exiled from Iceland for murder. The first Norse colonists were pagan, but Erik the Red's son, Leif, was converted to Catholic Christianity by King Olaf Trygvesson on a trip to Norway in 990 and sent missionaries back to Greenland.

On April 9, 1940, early during World War II, Denmark was occupied by Nazi Germany. On April 8, 1941, the United States occupied Greenland in order to defend it against a possible invasion by Germany. In 1946, the United States offered to buy Greenland for $100,000,000, but Denmark refused to sell. However, in 1950, Denmark agreed to allow the United States to re-establish Thule Air Base, which was gradually expanded 1951–1953 as part of a unified NATO cold war defence strategy.

7

Town of Flight's Origin

This true story originates out of BW-1 Narsarsuaq, Greenland. The short winter months had started to set in while a seven-man crew awaited clearance for their flight home, their first stop being Goose Bay, Labrador.

Records left behind in a diary state that, on November 12, 1942, these officers were ready to take their leave. Their hours of daylight were only about six hours from sunrise to sunset. Eighteen hours of darkness a day can become depressing, but it is something one lives with when in that environment. The B-26 was relatively a new plane. The crew had taken delivery of the plane in October 1942, which began its short life as a military plane.

Preparation for flight
That very night, the sky dropped a blanket of two inches

of snow, which seemed to lighten up the place. The crewmen commented that it looked pretty.

They spent most of the next morning trying to dust off the plane, hoping that they would be able to fly that day. As the day wore on, it seemed that they would be grounded again for another day.

Four days passed, and they still were waiting for clearance. The weather was unpredictable from day to day. Pilot Hodge and Co-pilot Jansen walked to a nearby river. It was a solid sheet of ice covered with about two inches of snow. As they walked over it, sometimes they would go through, as it wasn't thick enough in places to support their weight.

Crew of the B-26 *Time's A Wastin'*, which crashed in Saglek Bay

That night, the weather changed again, and with that change came rain. The winds picked up to around sixty miles per hour and brought with it a warm breeze.

After this mild spurt, most of the snow and ice but for a couple of patches were gone. Finally, after two weeks, the ground was nearly bare again.

On November 26, they were still waiting at the terminal for departure. The weather still wasn't the best, still overcast, but around 3:30 a.m., they got the call.

The crew got up and tried to kill some time until 6:00 a.m., when they would be briefed. They had to go through a rigorous inspection before takeoff.

As it turned out, they would have to wait another two weeks for departure.

8

Pre-Flight Procedure

1) Enter pilot's compartment to review maintenance items on Forms 1 and 1A, unlock controls, and check that all switches and levers are in off or neutral positions, and check navigation compartment, bomb bays, and rear sections of the aircraft for proper configuration. Check weight and balance of aircraft with the load adjuster.

2) Exit aircraft and perform a walk around to ensure the exterior of the aircraft looks satisfactory. Inspect each main gear and nose wheel opening for leaking fluid, strut condition, brake line's condition, and tire wear. Ensure all hatches are closed, gas filler caps are secured, pitot covers are removed, and then walk each propeller through for sixteen blades in direction of normal engine rotation.

3) Enter aircraft and ensure that fuel tank valves in forward bomb bay are turned on, that main inverter cut-off switch is turned on, that de-icer lever in navigation compartment is set to off, that bomb bay door selector handle in bombardier's compartment is in the closed position.

4) Move into pilot's seat, attach safety belt, check flight controls and trim tabs movement, close and lock overhead hatches, set parking brake, and pull brake lock on. Check that landing gear lever is down and locked, that pilot heater is off, that emergency air brake bleeder valve is off, that outside power source is connected to outlet in left nacelle, that master, ignition, and battery switches are off, that blowers are in low position, that oil cooler shutters are open, and that carburetor air control lever is in the cold position. Set mixture controls to idle cut-off, set propeller governor control levers full forward to increase rpm, set propeller toggle switches to auto constant speed and feather switches to normal, move cowl flap lever to open and then to neutral, and set inverter selector switch to on position. Check fuel gauge indicator level for all tanks.

5) For starting engines, turn battery switch on, set throttles approximately 3/4 inch open, clear propellers, notify ground crew, ensure fire guard is posted, turn master switch on, and turn left ignition switch to both magnetos. Switch left-hand booster pump on and prime left engine

for a few seconds. Hold energizer switch to left position until inertia flywheel reaches maximum rpm and turn primer switch on immediately prior to meshing the starter to the engine. Engage the starter to the engine by holding the mesh switch to the left position; at the same time, hold the primer switch down until engine starts, and then release both switches. When engine starts firing, move mixture controls to auto rich position. Manipulate the throttle to keep the engine running at 800 rpm initially, until there is an indicated oil pressure, and then increase to 1,000 rpm. Start the right engine in the same manner. Turn booster pumps off and disconnect auxiliary power source. Check hydraulic pressure for 800 to 1,050 pounds, set oil cooler shutters as required, and put carburetor air control levers in cold position. Adjust pilot's seat, tune radios, and contact control tower for taxi clearance and altimeter setting for airport pressure.

9
Takeoff and Landing Procedures

1) Taxi to takeoff position. Check brakes for proper functioning, check nose wheel for any shimmying characteristic, and position aircraft into the wind short of the runway for engine run-up checks. Move throttles to 1,700 rpm, pull propeller levers back to observe reduced rpm and then forward to obtain 1,700 rpm again. Move propeller toggle switches to decrease rpm, fixed pitch, increase rpm, and to constant speed rpm to observe proper functioning. Move throttles to 2,100 rpm and set toggle switch to fixed pitch, check left engine magnetos by moving switch to left magneto, then to both, then to right magneto, then back to both, and observe that there is not more than a drop of 75 rpm while doing this. Move toggle switch back to constant speed rpm position. Next, check right engine magnetos in the same way. Reduce throttles to 1,000 rpm and then clear engines by advancing each one to 2,700

rpm and observe temperature and pressure instruments to assure all are within green limits. Check operation of feathering switches. Lower flaps down to 1/4 position, turn booster pumps on, remove safety lock from landing gear lever, set trim tabs 5 degrees tail heavy for takeoff, and contact the tower for permission to move into takeoff position on the runway.

2) Position aircraft on the runway, release brakes, move throttles to 52 inches manifold pressure and 2,700 rpm, maintain directional control with coordinated brakes and then rudder control, raise nose wheel slightly off the runway at 80 mph and hold that altitude until aircraft lifts off runway. Raise landing gear immediately to obtain minimum single-engine airspeed of 140 mph as soon as possible, retract wing flaps at 500 feet and 170 mph, and set cowl flaps as required to maintain proper cylinder head temperature. Climb to desired altitude at 170 mph using 37 inches manifold pressure and 2,300 rpm, turn booster pumps off when levelling out, reduce power to 30 inches manifold pressure and 2,000 rpm for cruising, and move mixture controls to auto-lean when above 5,000 feet.

3) During the preparation for landing, the centre of gravity location should be checked if necessary using the load adjuster. Notify crew members to prepare for landing. Contact the airport tower to advise of landing intentions and obtain runway number in use, altimeter setting, wind

velocity and direction, and any caution notices. Set altimeter to station pressure, make sure blowers are in low position and safety cover is in place, adjust oil cooler shutters to maintain proper oil temperature, set carburetor air control levers to cold position, move mixture controls to auto rich when below 5,000 feet, set propeller toggle switches to auto constant speed and propeller levers to 2,250 rpm, turn fuel booster pumps on, reduce speed on downwind leg to 165 mph, place landing gear control lever in down position, and increase power to maintain 165 mph. Check wheel position indicator on pilot's instrument panel to show gear is down, locked, and in the green, and visually check to see that the landing gears are down.

4) Turn on final approach at 165 mph and lower flaps while reducing speed to 150 mph. Establish uniform rate of descent to runway. During "flare out," smoothly reduce power while pulling the nose up gradually for landing on the main wheels. After touchdown and speed is reduced, lower the nose wheel to the runway, leave cowl flaps open. Attach safety lock on landing gear lever, retract wing flaps, turn fuel booster pumps off, push propeller governor levers forward to increase rpm position, and taxi back to parking position.

Written by C. H. exclusively for B-26

10

Leaving for the United States

The weather now seemed to be getting worse. A few planes, such as the A-10s and the B-25s, started to kick off, but then shortly afterward it started to rain again, which lowered the cloud ceiling.

Their first stop was to be Goose Bay. Originally the *Time's A Wastin'* had been dispatched to England to provide aid for the British service.

After arriving in Greenland, the crew was ordered, for reasons not specified, to return to the USA.

About ten minutes later it stopped raining, and conditions looked fair, but it was now too late to take off.

Days seemed like weeks. They were anxious to leave. The passage of time from November 26 to December 10 seemed to take forever, but the day finally arrived.

On the morning of December 10, they lifted off for Goose Bay. What a feeling that must have been, after being quarantined for nearly a month. Everyone on board was excited at last to be going home.

Takeoff for a plane requires a few steps or procedures before it will rise from the ground. For example, a commercial airliner with a full load of people and baggage can usually lift off doing a speed of 160–180 mph. But it needs some kind of help to do so.

First of all, it requires airspeed. Airspeed is a measure of how fast the air is flowing over the plane.

If the plane is flying into a headwind, the airspeed will have to be increased. Airplanes normally take off facing into the wind.

Airspeed creates lift across the wings of the plane. A plane's wings have a curvature or camber that increases the distance the air has to travel over the top of the wings. In physics this is called the "Bernoulli effect." This principle states that as the pressure in air decreases, the speed of the air increases. Therefore, the faster the air over the top of the wings, the lower the pressure pushing down on the wing, and the difference created between the top and bottom of the wing creates a lift.

When preparing for takeoff, the pilot will lower the flaps on the wings of the plane. This increases the camber, which boosts the Bernoulli effect, helping to create more lift at lower airspeed.

The brakes are applied and the engines are then revved up in power, depending on the size and weight of the plane. When that set point is reached, the brakes are released and the plane starts to taxi down the runway. This again changes the airspeed over the top of the wings, and when it is high enough, the plane will lift off the ground. When in the air, the flaps are then retracted.

11

En Route to Goose Bay, Labrador

About ninety minutes into their flight, the *Time's A Wastin'* ran into some clouds. The pilot turned around to see what the other planes, which had already left before him, were going to do. One plane dropped out, and possibly another. The crew could barely discern their neighbours. They lost sight of them when they descended through the clouds.

Shortly, they saw an opening in the clouds to the south at about 2,000 feet. Flying in that direction, they finally broke out.

The sky now being clear, they decided to go back up to 13,000 feet elevation, where Navigator/Bombardier Second Lieutenant Emmanuel J. Josephson gave the pilot the nod to get back on course. From then on the flight went well, until they got about halfway to their destination.

The plane that they were flying was practically new. They had just taken delivery of this aircraft at Baer Field, Indianapolis, Indiana, in October 1942. One would not have expected any problems just yet. It was a Martin B-26 Marauder, a medium bomber of the 440th Squadron 319 Bomb Group.

History of the B-26 Marauder

On January 25, 1939, the US Army put out a request for bids on a new aircraft. From the specifications for speed, bomb load, and armament, it was clear that they wanted a medium bomber with pursuit ship speed. On July 5, 1939, the Glenn L. Martin Company of Baltimore, Maryland, was awarded the contract.

B-26 Marauder

Due to the growing intensity of the war in Europe, there was no time to build a prototype for testing. They had to take the first airplane off the production line and make it stand or fall on its merit. This first airplane came off the line in November 1940. The tests were satisfactory, and the plane was turned over to the army to be service tested.

In February 1941, the flow of planes to the army began. The first four, which made up the test fleet, flew 131 hours during the Accelerated Service Tests. Just three months later, these four airplanes were assigned to the 22nd Bomb Group at Langley Field, Virginia.

The early airplanes had what was then the highest wing loading of any military airplane. The cigar-shaped fuselage and stubby wings, powered by a pair of Pratt & Whitney R-2800-5 eighteen-cylinder engines, turning four-bladed Curtiss Electric hollow steel propellers, over thirteen feet in diameter, made it a most attractive and, at the same time, menacing sight. The armament at that time consisted of two .30-calibre machine guns, one each in the nose and tail, and twin .50-calibres in a Martin-designed power turret atop the fuselage. This armament grew with each design change, and by the time the 386th received their combat airplanes, they were bristling with .50-calibres, some models with as many as twelve guns, due to lessons learned during earlier combat experience in the Pacific theatre of war.

It was found, after experimenting with all the guns

and modifications added, that it was overloaded. By September 1942 the accident rate was so high that the safety board had to do an investigation to try and find the causes. It was the most maligned airplane ever built and was referred to as the flying brick. All of the planes assigned to the 386th had the longer wingspan of seventy-one feet, and a lengthened vertical fin for increasing control in single-engine emergencies.

Arriving at Selfridge—or Omaha, for those few who picked up their airplanes there—the 386th found that all had the longer wingspan—seventy-one feet—and many other refinements which were designed to make the Marauder an outstanding fighting machine. The vertical fin had been lengthened and four .50-calibre "package" guns were mounted, two on each side of the fuselage, firing forward. Some had Bell hydraulic power tail turrets in place of the twin flexible mount .50-calibre guns. All the bomb stations in the rear bomb bays had been removed and the doors sealed.

The bombardier's position in the Plexiglas nose held all the controls for the bomb doors and the bomb racks, provisions for a bomb sight, and a flexible .50-calibre machine gun. A few models also had a fixed .50-calibre firing forward. This fixed gun was generally removed after the 386th reached England.

A navigator's and radio operator's compartment, located just aft of the cockpit, provided space and facilities for the navigators and carried the long-range liaison radio.

A hatch which was equipped with an astrodome allowed sextant shooting for celestial navigation. It also provided a spot for a crew member to ride while taxiing in congested areas. He was thus able to clear the wing tips and the tail section and prevent collisions with other aircraft or fixed objects.

Flight engineers were often, although not always, the top turret gunners. The turret was equipped with firing interrupters, which prevented the guns from firing when pointed at any part of the B-26. The tail gunners were usually the armourers, and, as a rule, the radio operators operated the waist guns.

The pilot's compartment was arranged for side-by-side seating of the pilot and co-pilot. There was a tunnel in front of the co-pilot's seat which allowed the bombardier to enter and exit the nose section. Folding rudder pedals at the co-pilot's position made it easier for the bombardier to crawl through the tunnel.

Engine and propeller controls were located on a pedestal, between and forward of the two seats, accessible to either pilot. Landing gear and flap controls were also located on the pedestal, as were the aileron and elevator trim controls. The rudder trim was above the pedestal between the top hatches.

Fuel was carried in four tanks in the wings, two main and two auxiliary. It was necessary to transfer fuel from the auxiliaries to the mains, which then fed the engines. The main tank capacity was 360 gallons each, while the auxiliary held 121 gallons each, for a total of 962 gallons. For ferrying purposes, a pair of bomb bay tanks added another 500 gallons. During normal flight the flight engineer handled the fuel transfer, and in combat situations this job fell to the co-pilot. The transfer valves were located on the forward wall of the bomb bay.

The original design of the Model 179, which evolved over some four years into the B-26s of the 386th Group, made provisions for each of the crew members to accomplish his assigned tasks with the utmost efficiency. A look back from 1988 technology makes the B-26 look primitive. Primitive or not, it took its crews through many rough missions, achieving the lowest loss rate of any combat aircraft in World War II. The plane was hot and sometimes unpredictable, but to a man, the crews who flew the craft in combat loved it.

12

Purpose of the B-26 Marauder

The B-26 Marauder was designed to meet the US Army Air Corps' demand for a high-speed medium bomber. Martin's proposal was considered to be so far in advance of other proposals that the company was awarded an "off the drawing board" contract for 201 aircraft in 1939, and the first production B-26 flew by year's end. Testing confirmed that performance expectations had been achieved but at the expense of low-speed handling characteristics. Training accidents multiplied, and an investigation was set up to consider whether or not production should be stopped. It was decided to introduce modifications that would improve the plane's slow-speed handling qualities.

Later aircraft were built with longer wings, a lengthened fuselage, and larger vertical fin and rudder. B-26s saw combat in the South Pacific as well as in North Africa.

Over 5,000 Marauders were built, and it went on to have the lowest combat attrition rate of any American aircraft in the 9th Air Force.

Specifications changed with each model. The airplanes that the 386th took to combat were of approximately the following specifications:

Wingspan 71 feet
Length 58 feet 6 inches
Height (top of fin) 20 feet 4 inches
Wing Area 658 square feet
Empty Weight 24,000 pounds
Maximum Gross Weight 38,200 pounds
Wing Loading 49 pounds per square feet
Maximum Airspeed 323 mph
Cruise Airspeed 230 mph
Service Ceiling 21,500 feet
Combat Radius 575 miles
Maximum Bomb Load 5,200 pounds
    (20–260 pound frag. bombs)
Normal Bomb Load 4,000 pounds
Ferry Range 2,000 miles
Normal Crew 6
Armament 12 .50-calibre machine guns
Engines 2 P&W R-2800-43 18-cylinder radial
Fuel 100–130 octane aviation grade
Maximum Power 2,000 HP at 2,700 rpm & 51 in. Hg.

Only six B-26s still exist, and only one capable of flight. Because of its small wing area, the B-26 was nicknamed the "Widowmaker." MacDill Air Force Base in Tampa was the main training base for B-26 crews during the war. As a result of a short series of training accidents after takeoff, the undeserved phrase "One a day in Tampa Bay" came about.

Their first scheduled stop of the *Time's A Wastin'* en route to the United States was to be the base in Goose Bay, which had just opened that summer. The Americans were busy at that site. It was a fuelling base for the many planes that were coming and going at the time. Even today, that base is still being used as a station for fuelling, cold-weather flight testing, and also low-level flight testing. A reminder of its military past, such as the airport and dorms, is still in existence.

Labrador is notorious for its plane crashes, but there is one accident that landed it a spot in the province's archaeological history. Until the writing of this book, few people knew about it.

13

The Russian Submarine *Kursk 141*

It has been said time and time again that history repeats it-self. A story of note is that of the Russian submarine *Kursk* (*K141*), which had an explosion on board August 12, 2000. The *Kursk* was a nuclear-powered cruise missile submarine of the Russian Navy. It was named after the Russian city Kursk.

Kursk submarine (*K141*), which had an explosion on board August 12, 2000

This submarine was 154 metres (505.2 feet) long, with a beam of 18.2 metres (60 feet) and draft 9 metres (29.5 feet). It could travel at 32 knots (59 kmh) (32 mph) when submerged and 16 knots (30 kmh) (18 mph) when surfaced.

This submarine was on a training exercise, which was to have been the largest summer drilling, nine years after the Soviet Union's collapse. The exercise involved four attack submarines, the fleet's flagship, *Pyotr Velikiy*, and a flotilla of smaller ships.

The *Kursk* sortied out on an exercise to fire dummy torpedoes at the Kirov Class battle cruiser *Pyotr Velikiy*. The practice torpedoes had no explosive warheads and had been tested to a much lower-quality standard.

On August 12, 2000, there was an explosion while preparing to fire. Some sources suggest that the cause of detonation was the *Kursk's* hydrogen peroxide–fuelled Type 65 torpedoes. The highly concentrated hydrogen peroxide seeped through rust in the torpedo casing. The explosion produced a blast equal to 220–550 pounds (100–250 kilograms) of TNT, after which the sub then sank in a shallow body of water 108 metres (354 feet) deep. A second explosion one minute and thirty-five seconds later produced a blast much larger than the first. It blew a large piece of debris back through the submarine.

This submarine carried a total of 118 sailors and officers, and all perished. There has been much debate over how long the sailors or officers might have survived, as

THE DIARY OF ONE NOW DEAD

some soldiers had time to write notes confirming that they lived for a short while after.

One such note found on a body by a recovery worker showed that twenty-three sailors (out of 118 on board) had waited in the dark with him, hoping to be rescued.

The Russian Admiralty at first thought that most of the crew died within minutes of the explosion, but the recovery proved otherwise. According to the time on one note, it appeared that some sailors lived at least four hours after the explosion.

Given the amount of time, it was possible that the sailors could have been rescued, had a rescue plan been implemented immediately. America, Britain, and Norway offered their services, but Russia declined their offers. Thirty-two hours later, an attempt was made to try and rescue the workers, but by then it was too late.

The sailors who gathered together in the aft compartment were there in the dark until eventually the fire, as a result of the explosion, used up all the oxygen in the air. They were prisoners on their own ship and, like the crew of the *Time's A Wastin'*, time was not on their side. All aboard the *Kursk* died from asphyxiation due to carbon monoxide poisoning.

No one came to their aid, and thus closed the chapter on another preventable tragedy.

14

Crossing the Davis Strait

Their flight path took them across the Davis Strait, a distance of 1,309 kilometres (814 miles). At that time, these waters were probably infested with German U-boats. Many people didn't know what the Germans were up to, but much later, after the crash, it was learned that the Germans had established a weather station in Northern Labrador. According to some sources, it was the only known such station to be set up in North America. If that was the case, the Germans would have known about this site for a long time.

The day the crew left to fly, everything on board was in good working order, and they felt safe in this fairly new plane.

Approaching Newfoundland and Labrador
After flying for about 600 kilometres, they made contact with Goose Bay, where they would make their first stop.

But just a few minutes later, they lost radio contact. Their radio went dead, and repeated attempts to resurrect it proved unsuccessful. They discovered that their batteries had gone dead and, sad to say, they didn't have any spares on board.

At the time, radio silence was crucial so as to not give away one's location to the enemy. Most everyone living in outport Newfoundland and Labrador was required to place blinds or blankets over any windows, to prevent any light from getting out. This security measure served to hide the occupied communities and thus avoid giving enemies flying overhead reason to attack.

On one occasion, the evening the author's mother got married, she recalls that, after they had left the church to go into the lodge for their reception, a plane flew low overhead and made a circle, shining its spotlight on her and the bridespeople. The aircraft circled with its light on them until they went into the reception lodge, and then it flew away.

According to Max Peddle, a retired sergeant and also the museum's curator at the air force base in Goose Bay, says that when the crew of the *Time's A Wastin'* sent out their initial radio signal, they were in fact talking to a German U-boat that was secretly patrolling the waters off the Davis Strait. The Germans had their U-boats, and sometimes ships, in these waters of the North Atlantic, where they were pitted against the Allies during transatlantic runs. Sailing those waters was dangerous. Once they set sail, everyone was basically on his own. Military records don't mention anyone communicating with any aircraft trying to make contact with Goose Bay that time, so it would stand to reason that they were more than likely intercepted by the Germans.

For the remaining part of their flight, they navigated by compass under a sky that was cloud-covered, which threw them off course. Clouds were now becoming a concern, and they became the subject of their conversation. The crewmen must have been asking themselves how far were they from land, and from Goose Bay. The crewmen knew how long it was going to take, and now they were a little over halfway to their destination. They started to worry.

Was there any point in returning back to Greenland? The thought must have crossed their minds. How low were the clouds, and how high was the coastline? If they continued in the clouds, it was possible that they could go way off course, or, if too low, they ran the risk of striking land. But as they flew closer, the clouds lifted a little and they could finally see where they were going. That was a great relief, but they were far from safe.

Once they knew they were in sight of land, their courage was renewed. The wide-open waters of the Davis Strait and the ensuing winds that beat against the plane shook them as they moved forward inland toward Goose Bay. But it wasn't long before they discovered they were off course and that their destination was nowhere to be found.

As they neared the coast of Labrador, they made a guess as to their location and, judging from the steep cliffs, they figured they were flying too far south, so they decided to alter their course to take them farther to the north. They didn't know that they were already flying north of Goose Bay and the change in direction shifted them farther north again.

After flying inland for a short period of time, they realized that the plane was nearly out of fuel. It was decided that they had no other choice but to find a suitable place to crash-land, as they knew they were not going to reach their destination.

15

Preparing to Crash-Land

They surveyed the area in a sharp, low circle, looking eagerly for the best of the frozen, rough tundra to ditch the plane. They would have preferred a place where there were trees so it would give them a smoother landing, but the landscape was all barren ground and rocks. The engines started to miss, and that was their cue to bring her down.

All the crew were made aware that they were going to perform an emergency landing, and each man prepared himself. Circling around, the pilot picked out a place not far from the coastline. There may have been better places to land, but a decision had to be made immediately.

As the plane made its descent, all the crew braced for the worst. There were a lot of things that could go wrong: the plane could explode and catch on fire; the propellers of the plane could come off and cut into the plane, causing injuries; they could be thrown from the plane. These and other scenarios had to be taken into consideration.

Pilot Hodge gave the plane a bumpy but smooth landing with the aid of Second Lieutenant Emanuel J. Josephson, navigator/bombardier, who helped kill the switch to shut power to the engines. It was smooth in the sense that no one really got hurt, but the plane itself suffered some damage. As it skidded over the frozen hillside, it struck a rock protruding from the ground. It swung around almost ninety degrees, then came to an abrupt stop, but not before tearing the bomb bay open and sending one of the propeller tips through the fuselage. The plane's position shielded the men from the wind.

Luckily, no one was injured aside from a few scratches. It was a cruel way to be introduced to the cold north of Labrador, but at least everyone survived the crash. Few people can boast of living through incidents such as this.

When the plane had completely stopped, everyone was ordered to bail out. This was a precaution, in case the plane exploded following the impact. If there was a small leak in the fuel line and there was still fire in the engines, an explosion could occur.

A survey of the plane from the outside revealed that it was still fully intact. The crew didn't realize that this would be their home for the rest of their lives.

It was almost dark when they decided to have a cold lunch and retire for the night.

Lieutenant Josephson scanned the skies and figured that they were about 300 minutes from Goose Bay.

On board they had seventeen blankets, a comforter, and a bedroll. Even though they had no heat, they slept through the night.

16

Plan for Survival

The first day after the crash, December 11, navigator/ bombardier Lieutenant Josephson and Corporal Frank Golm walked to fjords, one to the east and the other to the west. They were scouting out the area to figure out their options. Lieutenant Josephson, in the end, would be one of three who would volunteer their lives to set out in boat to look for help.

That day, the men started to organize the plane and gather the food that had scattered upon impact. Their supply of food consisted of cans of Spam, chicken, peanuts, crackers, cookies, and chocolates. They checked out the surrounding environment and found a lake where a small supply of wildlife roamed.

They tried to establish radio contact again, but it was too late. The batteries were dead. Judging from the sky and their charts, they determined that they were close to the small community of Hebron. If they were to travel to the mountain and saw nothing, what then? They would have to try and make it back again before any weather came on. It was a gamble. The men debated many times whether to make the trip or not, but because of the cold, uncertainty as to which route to take, snow, brightness of the sun, and lack of warm clothing, they elected to stay with the plane in case someone found them.

As the sun sank beyond the horizon each day, they wondered what the next day would bring, or when the sun would rise again. They tried to believe that it would bring them good news.

Name: Frank J. Golm
Born: Sep 7, 1907, New York
Residence: Bronx, New York
Enlisted: Dec 19, 1941
Service Number: 12037633
Rank: Private/Corporal
Military Occupation: Radio Operator
Civil Occupation: Salesman and Sales Agent
Marital Status: Married
Burial: Plot H, Lot 7680, Long Island National Cemetery, Farmingdale, Suffolk County, New York

17

Getting Settled In

The crew of the *Time's A Wastin'* looked out each morning at the bright blue sky, not knowing what to expect. Some may have even written a note and let it slip into the air, hoping that the wind would take it and eventually someone would find it and conduct a search. They must have placed markings of some bright colours on the wings of the plane which would be visible from the air should someone fly overhead. It is not known whether they had any flares on board. However, even if they had, they wouldn't have been much use, given that they were so far away from a community.

These few bright, sunny days were torturous with the cold. Before long the sun would disappear beyond the horizon for another eighteen hours, and then the air would become bitterly cold.

The crewmen were hoping for a rescue, but now their

hopes were starting to wane. Some nights they could hear the sound of a jetliner and see its faint lights flashing as it sped across the clear sky.

There were days when jets passed overhead, leaving just a trail of white vapour to slowly dissipate into the thin air above, their passengers unaware of the dangerous predicament that these men were in. The days must have seemed like weeks. They couldn't wait for the sun to go down, and they couldn't wait for it to rise again.

There were days when the howling winds and blowing snow prevented them from going outside. The body heat from each person was hardly enough to keep themselves warm. When they did make it outside, they had a difficult job of trying to keep the plane free from snow in the event someone was trying to locate them from the air. If the plane was snowed in, they would never be found.

The cold nights left a blanket of frost on the ground that just crunched beneath their feet. They needed to be well dressed, especially with good boots, to withstand those frigid temperatures. Sometimes they would go outside to warm up. Metal stores a lot of cold, so at times it was probably a lot warmer on the outside than inside.

18

Time to Plan Their Strategy

The first two weeks after their landing were gruesome. They were now starting to get desperate. The crew figured that two weeks should have been long enough for someone to realize that they were lost or had gone down and try and send a search party.

Something had to be done soon, or else everyone was going to die. They consulted with each other and finally made a decision. A plan was quickly put in place for three men to take the emergency boat, which was part of their emergency survival kit, and row south along the coastline to look for help.

At 7:15 a.m. on December 23, just thirteen days after the crash, they got up, readied the boat, and left. The three crewmen—Navigator/Bombardier Second Lieutenant Emmanuel J. Josephson, Jr., Co-pilot Second Lieutenant Paul Jansen, and Radio Operator Technical

Sergeant Charles F. Nolan—headed south in their small boat.

The details of this story come from the journal entries of one of the crew members involved in the crash, namely the pilot, First Lieutenant Grover Cleveland Hodge. It is a daily diary of the men's attempt to survive in an unforgiving land.

Name: Paul W. Jansen

From: Minnesota

Service Number: 0-727881

Rank: Second Lieutenant, 440 AAF BOMB SQ, 319 BOMB GP WORLD WAR II

Service: US Army Air Forces

Regiment: 440th Bomber Squadron, 319th Bomber Group

War: World War II

Military Occupation: Co-pilot

Burial: Missing in Action or Buried at Sea, Tablets of the Missing at East Coast Memorial, New York City, USA (East Coast Memorial, Manhattan, New York)

Name: Charles F. Nolan

From: New York, New York

Service Number: 32174825

Rank: Sergeant, Squadron, 319th Bomber Group, Medium

War: World War II

Service: US Army Air Forces

Regiment: 440th Bomber Squadron, 319th Bomber Group

Burial: Missing in Action or Buried at Sea, Tablets of the Missing at East Coast Memorial, New York City, USA (East Coast Memorial, Manhattan, New York)

As far as we know, Sergeant Nolan was a passenger on this plane, as stated earlier, that had been dispatched to England but afterwards was told to return to the USA.

Note: The 319th Bombardment Group trained in Louisiana in B-26 Marauders, and after completing initial training in November 1942, the group reported to the Mediterranean theatre of operations, where it was assigned to the 12th Air Force.

In October and November 1942, it moved to Algeria as the first B-26 unit in that theatre, entering combat for the first time on November 28.

The Journey to Reach the Sea

The wind was blowing strong that day, and it hampered the aviators' progress. As they made their way across the open tundra, there were times when the wind almost took their breath away.

By noon they had finally succeeded in reaching the edge of a cliff, where lay a deep precipice. They tied a rope to the boat and gradually lowered it down the steep embankment. This took some time, as the slope was dangerous and slippery.

The runoff water from the top made its way over the 1,800-foot drop and formed ice as it found its way down to the sea. One slip could prove to be fatal.

The cliff provided a spectacular view from the hillside, but for the mariner it presented many dangers. The plane *Time's A Wastin'* had crashed in an area that offered no mercy to those who traversed it: this kind of territory; so far north, consisted of open barrens and low land. Given the time of the year, the terrain was near-impassable to human travellers.

Labrador has been called many things, such as "the land God gave to Cain" and "the Big Land." It is also known for its cold temperatures. The land is much colder than western Canada due to its dampness and wind chill. When temperatures are sixty to seventy degrees below zero, one can only leave his gloves off for about thirty seconds for fear of freezing.

It is not known how the three men descended the steep embankment. One can only speculate on the few options they had. They may have been let down by a rope, much the same way as they had lowered the boat to the water. Another option would have been to find a spot near the coastline that wasn't as steep and inch their way down to the water and their waiting vessel. After the boat was in the water, they exchanged farewells with the remaining four men and prayed that they would have a safe trip and that they would be able to find help. As they pushed off from the steep, rugged cliff, they rowed hard to get away from the swell that was throwing itself against the shoreline and to weave out through the slob ice, toward the open water.

How far they travelled no one will ever know, as they were never heard tell of after. Whether the high winds and strong currents sent them drifting farther north, or their boat struck some sharp rocks and turned over or sank, will forever remain a mystery. It is also possible they were sunk by a submarine, as these waters were swarming with German U-boats at the time.

19

Business as Usual

Back at the plane, some of the remaining four endured injuries to their feet that needed tending, probably due to the impact of the crash. Their home now was inside the plane. Their blankets were frozen and had to be thawed. Food supplies were starting to run low.

Before the others had departed in the boat, food had to be shared with them for their survival. How much food was given them we will never know, but they received their share. Inventory would have to be taken very soon to see how much longer they could go before rationing.

There was a lot going on in the minds of these men, especially so close to Christmas. In their hearts they really believed that they would be rescued, and what kept them going was hope. Of course, after two weeks, their faith started to become tested. Watching the sun rise and set each day was not very exciting, but it renewed their strength to look forward to another day.

20

Christmas Holidays

Christmas Eve came, December 24, and by now two weeks had passed. It was lonely, especially with the other three gone, but the remaining four got up and tried to get a fire going from a gas container they had dug out. The winds were high that day, and they couldn't do much outside the plane, so they decided to dry out their blankets.

Corporal Frank J. Golm had blisters on his hands, and they started to swell and get worse. From then on he had to treat them carefully so as not to get them infected. They made the best of the day by stretching out their eating, to make the day not seem so long.

That day, each person had a can of herring with crackers, a spoonful of peanuts, a black cough drop, a caramel, a can of grape drink, and plenty of coffee, using the same grounds over and over.

Christmas morning arrived. They thought they would

have been home by now, but they had to come to grips with reality. The cold wind continued to bite through their winter apparel, and they realized their peril was all too real.

James J. Mangini, Jr., who was one of the gunners, had hurt his feet when they crashed. He woke the others around 3:30 a.m. They had to get up and rub his feet to give him some relief. The pain was unbearable at times. After they massaged his feet for a while, he fell asleep. The others retired until around 9:00 a.m. Everyone but Pilot Hodge had some form of injury.

Name: James J. Mangini, Jr.

Serial Number: 12077708

State: New Jersey

County: Bergen

Rank: Private

Branch: Warrant Officers

Army: Army of The United States - Voluntary Enlistments

Birth Year: 1917

Enlist Date: April 27, 1942

Enlistment Place: Newark, New Jersey

Term: Duration of War, plus six months

Nativity: New Jersey

Race: White

Citizenship: Citizen

Education: Four years high school

Civilian Occupation: Unskilled occupations in production of asbestos, abrasives, and polishing products

Marital Status: Single

Dependents: No dependents

Enlistment Source: Civilian

Conflict Period: World War II

Golm, also a gunner, decided to take a little tour around the site while Gunner Sergeant Russell Weyrauch started fixing up the floor. It was in bad shape due to a fire that had started in the plane upon landing. Debris lay all around the site. In order to fix up the window, they had to dig out the entryway to the plane.

After they had their Christmas dinner of rations, they went to bed. Christmas day came and went, and by the next day the weather had cleared. Golm did a little digging around the rear of the bomb bay and uncovered a can of chicken a la king and a can of fruit cocktail.

Hodge Worked on Mangini's feet again and did a few more chores around the site. Everyone's spirits were up a little, but concern for Mangini's feet was on their minds. They couldn't afford to lose anyone due to an infection.

For the next five to six days, to the end of the year, they made the best they could of a bad situation. Mangini's feet improved a little, but an eye had to be kept on him as a blister appeared on each foot. It is not known how he got the blisters. They could have come as the result of frostbite, or from his damp socks chafing against his boots. To prevent him from getting a chill, they had to dry out their blankets every day. One day, they climbed a small mountain to see if they could see anything out to sea, but they saw nothing for miles around.

Sgt. Russell Weyrauch, Engineer/Air Gunner

It stands to reason that, had they known how long they were going to be stranded, they would have made an attempt to make it to the hills nearby. If for nothing else but to satisfy their curiosity. It would have been just as bad for them to die on the mountain trying to find an escape route than to sit with the plane and die of starvation.

Some days the winds were high and they stayed inside the plane all day. Food supplies were getting lower all the time, and they were starting to become discouraged. Had the weather been a little warmer, events may have unfolded differently.

Sometime between December 29 and December 30

there is another diary entry. What follows is a lengthy, somewhat incoherent, and rambling discourse in a different handwriting, apparently the entry of someone other than Pilot Hodge. In this entry, the writer is obviously despondent and thinking of his wife or sweetheart. He dwells on the "taste" and "message" and "warmth" of kisses; the satisfaction, even, in "rubbing noses."

Yet, if the taste of kisses went and strawberries came the year round, half of the joy would be gone from the world. There is no wonder we kiss for when mouth comes to mouth in all its stillness, breath joins breath, and taste joins taste. Warmth is enwarmed, and tongues can move in a soundless language, and those things are said that cannot be said, have a name or know a life in the pitiful faults of speech. There is nothing to be done with the ear, so back we come to the organs of taste and smell. It is temple of the voice, keeper of the breath, treasures of tastes and home of the noble tongue. And its portals are firm, yet soft with the warmth of a ripeness unlike the rest of the face, rosy and in women with a conkling red tenderness of the taste, not to compare with the wild strawberry feeling and far from the organs of taste and smell, and far from the brain, and an arm's length from the heart. To rub a nose like the blacks and it is better than nothing at all, but there is nothing to the taste about the nose, only an old piece of bone pushing out of the face, and a nuisance in time of winter, but a friend before meals and in a garden indeed. With the eye we can do nothing, for if we come too close they become crossed and everything comes twice and sight without good for one or all five, no angles with a fluring world yet this it was that left the grapes to weed. I had eaten of the tree. Eve was still warm under me. There is strange and yet not strange in the kiss; it is strange because it mixes stillness with tragedy and yet not strange because there is good reason for it. The hand is too hard and too used to doing all things with too little, and deeper and closer.

December 30 came with no sign of rescue. The three crewmen who had left by boat had now been gone for a week. The remaining men were sure they would have heard something by now.

Things were looking grim. In the mornings when they awoke, they would look out through the portholes of the plane and scan the area for any signs of movement before going outside to start their daily chores. The metal of the plane didn't emit much in the way of odours which could attract any wildlife.

The remaining crew in the plane were beginning to doubt they were going to make it. The second-last day of the year dawned with overcast skies and some snow flurries. All the crew worked inside the plane again that day. Golm lost a fingernail, and by the looks of things, he could lose another.

21

New Year's Day

It appears that no one wrote in the diary on December 31. We don't know why. Perhaps the men were feeling helpless.

January 1 dawned, and the sound of "Happy New Year" rang throughout the small living quarters of the plane. There wasn't much to be happy about, but they had to try and keep up their morale. It snowed all through the pre-dawn hours of the morning and all day, and the wind caused heavy whiteouts. The crew had nothing they could use to start a fire with, so to keep warm they stayed in bed all day. Their beds were only makeshift bunks with just enough blankets to go around.

Survival Mode

The weather wasn't much better the next day, January 2: more snow and wind. Someone lit a little fire in a peanut can, just enough to know there was a fire. They all got up around noon and managed to drain some oil from the tank, and that was the extent of the heat they had.

After they had some hot coffee, lemon powder, and a cup of bullion, they had their main dish, which consisted of a date roll with jelly, and they seemed to love it. It was noon by the time they had finished eating and drinking. They were still optimistic about the boys who had left in the small boat. They were hoping to be rescued at any moment.

Another day passed and although it seemed that the wind had died out, it picked up again in the afternoon and started to snow once more. By now the body of the plane had a sheet of ice on it and was covered with snow.

As they rushed to get some fuel from the fuel transfer pump, some gas spilled over the side and ignited. Upon close examination, they discovered that the writer of the diary had gotten burnt a little, but nothing serious. It wasn't a pretty sight to see your own crewmate full of bandages.

Somehow they managed to do a few chores around the plane. They banked snow under the beds to fill a large hole that had lain open due to the crash. The snow acted as an insulator and prevented the wind from coming in.

Today was the eighth consecutive day with severe weather. There really wasn't much to get up for and to keep their spirits alive. They puttered around at a few small things, just to keep occupied. The men tried to retrieve the remaining fuel in the wings to provide them with a little heat and light.

With each new batch of snow, a couple of them would clean off the plane to allow anyone flying overhead to see them. It seemed that when the weather started, it could be bad for a week or more. The entrance of the plane became blocked with snow at the beginning of every day, no matter how many times they cleaned it off.

Four weeks had passed, but it seemed much longer. Monotony was now a part of their daily routine. Eat, sleep, and do a little work.

One morning they awakened to find some small tracks in the snow. To their surprise, they saw a small white bird. It must have gone off course, but it was right on course for those men. They managed to lure this bird, probably a partridge, close enough to catch it. They got the pot out and made a soup.

Food was running low, but it can go far when it is rationed. They prayed daily that God would help them get out of their dilemma. Was this bird an omen?

For the first time in thirteen days, Mangini finally got outdoors. His feet were well enough to brave the elements once more. The men were anxious to find the town of Hebron, but they never made a conscious effort to locate it. Of course it would be dangerous to try, given the soft snow and the risk of developing snow blindness.

Since the time of the crash on December 10, they had made no attempt to discover where Hebron lay. Time was now taking its toll, and these men were getting weaker every day from lack of food. The pilot, Hodge, started to check out his surroundings, but he didn't get too far. Before long, he encountered two mountains in front of him. What lay beyond each mountain was anyone's guess, so he decided to turn back.

22

Hoping to Be Rescued

It was coffee that kept them going from day to day. They would sip on that and talk of things like food and how good it would be to return home for a cooked meal. They worked on the putt-putt radio for some time, and at one point they thought they had it working. If they could get a signal out, they would have a chance of being rescued, but each time it continued to jam.

One month had passed. It was a miracle they had survived this long. Weather conditions were not great, and the sleeping quarters were nothing to be desired, but they kept going. Other times, the weather co-operated. If anyone was out searching for them, they could have easily spotted them as they made sure that the plane was always visible.

Everyone still remained optimistic as they worked around the outside of the plane. From time to time they would have a church service to keep their spirits alive.

One day, the only food that they ate was a slice of pineapple and two spoonfuls of juice. It wasn't much to look forward to.

The New Year had brought cold weather. Normally, with colder temperatures, one doesn't get much snow. It is only when the temperatures warm up that it starts to snow. January always seems to be the coldest. This kind of cold weather was ideal for anyone doing search and rescue, for the skies were mostly clear, and one could see if a plane was coming from either direction. Every day they watched the skies for the plane that never came.

Hope was now starting to dwindle, but they never gave up, even though they were getting weaker and weaker with each passing day.

The next day was overcast again, but there was no wind. The crewmen took the opportunity to dig up the oil and light a small fire to dry out their blankets. They made a spread on the snow and ate their meal, which consisted of a slice of Spam and a soda cracker for each of the four. The meal left for the next day was half a pound of chocolate and three drink powders. It wasn't good to think beyond that.

January 14, 1943, proved another great day with blue skies, but a little windy. They cleaned off the plane again, still hoping someone would see them.

While playing a game of cards to pass the time, Mangini tried to add more gas to the fire. He poured it on a little too fast and there was an explosion, which caused burns to his face, hair, and hands.

The ration for that day was four chocolates, but they never complained.

Every night before they went to sleep, they had a devotional and asked God to help them and provide a way out for them. Even though things were looking bleak, in their hours of loneliness and desperation they were still making plans for a couple of days in New York once they were rescued.

Another small ration meal and then they would try to get to bed again. Even though they never felt really hungry from how little they were eating, it wasn't enough protein to keep them strong. Every day their bodies were becoming weaker and weaker because they weren't producing enough heat and energy.

One day, it was so cold that the oil froze. Normally oil doesn't freeze, but there was probably a certain amount of condensation in it. After that they had to rely on burning gas. This would be their last meal together unless help arrived soon. The meal consisted of one bouillon powder and two sticks of gum.

January 18 started off as just another day, cold and clear. Hodge's watch gave out, and they didn't get up until noon. Today was going to be their first day without food, but their spirits were still high. In their hearts they were still hoping that someone would find them, although they didn't know how much longer they could go on.

January 19 was another day when nothing was written in the diary.

The next day, the snow never let up. It continued all night and grew windy. The men had gotten a good night's sleep and seemed to be a little happier. It was a job in itself trying to keep the snow away from the door of the plane; if they didn't dig out regularly, the plane would be covered with snow and would become invisible. They wanted to keep the plane exposed as much as possible.

January 21. Surviving for six weeks stranded on a cold, barren land was indeed quite a feat. Four days after their last meal, it rained and snowed and everything was soaked with water when they got up. One man stayed in bed while Hodge and Weyrauch got up long enough to melt some snow for water. Water had become their only diet. It sustained them for a while.

They spent a long and miserable night that night as the four of them seemed crowded and uncomfortable.

They made the best of the day, considering the fact that the outlook now seemed grim. They kept talking and tried to encourage each other, but each man knew they couldn't go on much longer. They would start something and not have the strength to finish it.

The days came and went. Another day of optimism, but also another day closer to the end.

On January 24, the pilot wrote in his diary for the last time for that month. That day started out a little overcast but with little wind. They were living their lives now one day to the next. That day the four of them smoked a pipe of tobacco. Golm couldn't take it—it made him sick, probably due to an empty stomach.

23

Hope Starting to Vanish

For the next few days, they all slept in bed. There was nothing to get up for, and there was not much point in shovelling anymore.

A few days earlier, Weyrauch hadn't been feeling well and, as a result, developed a case of the piles. After spending a full week in bed, he died as a result of his illness. It was too much for him to fight off, and he passed away, leaving just Golm, Hodge, and Mangini alone.

February 3 was the last entry in the diary. It seemed to close the chapter of the entire crew. Did the other three die the same day? We will never know.

Looking back on their lives, would it have been better if they had all died in the crash rather than go through such an ordeal?

24

Testimony of Christine Baikie

After a long time of searching, and finding no leads on the story of the crew of the *Time's A Wastin'*, I decided to call Nain, Labrador. I had emailed a person in that community a year or so before and received no reply.

I called the town council office in Nain, figuring that if anyone knew anything about the plane crash, it would be the town itself, but I was disappointed. I talked to a lady for a while, and she said it was best to call the radio station. If anyone knew anything about the crash of the *Time's A Wastin'*, it would be the radio people. She gave me their phone number and I made the call.

After talking to this lady for a while and explaining to her what I was looking for, in the end she shared the same news to me as the lady at the town hall. But before hanging up, she asked me for my number and said she would get back to me if she found out anything. To my surprise, within an hour I received a phone call from an elderly lady in Nain.

Christine Baikie informed me she'd had a call from the radio station. This lady, now eighty-three years old, along with her sister, who was two years younger, were the two oldest surviving residents of Hebron, Labrador, at the time.

She told me that she was only a small girl at the time but could remember her father telling her the story of the crash. Her father was one of the people who helped remove the bodies after the crash of the *Time's A Wastin'* was discovered. She then start to relate to me what she could remember.

Christine Baikie

In late fall of 1942, some Inuit people were out duck hunting and also trying for a seal to provide food for their families. At that time of the year, the ice was loose and usually slushy. Sometimes this can be a dangerous occupation, mainly because of the ice, and jumping from pan to pan, one slip and you are gone into the frigid waters. If there is no one there to help you get out, it could be fatal. I know this from experience, as I had spent two springs off the coast of Labrador with the well-known and famed sealing captain Morrissey Johnson in his famous sailing ship *Lady Johnson*.

The Inuit hunters ended up in the Davis Strait that day, where they figured they would find the most birds. They picked up a couple of seals, but the ice was heavily packed together and a lot of slush had gathered, leading right to the shoreline. Visibility was fair, and the weather was a typical day for that time of the year.

As they moved around the straits trying to find more birds and seals, they noticed something they had never seen before on top of the hillside. The object appeared to be large and dark. They weren't close enough to make out what it was, and they would have tried to go to land to find out what it was, but for the ice. The shoreline was packed with slob ice, and even if they could make it to land, they would never have been able to scale the 1,800-foot precipice that lay ahead. The hillside had ice from the top of the plain to the bottom.

Before heading back home that evening, they tried

to get closer to take one last look at this object. The more they looked, the more they were convinced that this object was unusual. Although they had viewed this hillside many times before, they knew that this was something different.

As they left for home that evening, the strange-looking object filled their thoughts. When they pulled in to their community, everyone was glad to see that they had a good catch. After they tied up their boat, people gathered at the wharf to help them with their catch and with the skinning of the seals. When the hunters got straightened away and cleaned up, they went to the Newfoundland ranger and the Moravian minister, whose name was Reverend Siegfried P. Hettasch, and reported their findings. Both the ranger and the reverend were surprised and thought that it was worth checking out. The Moravians did great work in Hebron, and for their accomplishments the old church, where they once went to worship, has been fully restored and stands today as a great testimony to their work.

Given the fact that winter had now arrived, nothing was done right away to explore what the hunters had seen. Later, in the spring of 1943, a couple more Inuit hunters set out by dogsled to set some traps and do a little hunting. As they travelled the barren country, they came across what the sealers had reported to the ranger and the reverend.

The first thing they saw was the wing of a plane. Nothing seemed to be moving. There didn't seem to be any life anywhere, and it appeared that the plane had a tarpaulin over it. After taking a full view of the scene, one hunter decided to pull the tarpaulin aside a little to see what was underneath. To their surprise, they discovered what looked like a man's hand. That was enough for them to determine what had happened. They called out to see if they could get any response, but silence greeted them. They knew then that there were no survivors. After carefully placing the tarpaulin over the plane again, they headed back home.

Back in Hebron, no one was expecting bad news of any kind. There were no reports of any planes or talk of any people missing. Not long after the hunters returned, the ranger and the reverend were made aware of their findings. One of the hunters gained access to a communications device and by way of Morse code sent a message to St. John's, notifying the proper authorities of their discovery. A few days later, a plane equipped with skis landed on the frozen ice in the harbour of Hebron. The plane carried three American officers—Major Vaughan, Lieutenant Holmes, and Lieutenant Norton—who were to travel to the crash site and conduct an investigation.

The officers arranged for a couple of dog teams to assist them in their recovery operation. According to Christine Baikie her father, Sam Lyall, and her uncle were two of the team leaders who assisted them. When the weather was suitable to travel, the group left for the crash site. Early in the morning, as it started to get daylight, the tackled dogs and the search teams headed in the direction where the sealers had seen the dark object. They had to travel somewhere between fifteen to eighteen miles.

Sam Lyall

After travelling for a few hours, they finally reached the crash site. The tarpaulin still covered the plane as was reported by the previous hunters. They quickly discovered that the plane was in good shape, so they slowly removed the covering to give them access inside. Not knowing what to expect, they cautiously proceeded to enter the close quarters where the men had spent the last few months of their lives. To their surprise, the inside of the plane was black with smoke. Whatever they were burning had eventually turned the inside a sooty black.

According to Christine Baikie, her father said that

Lady Johnson

when they discovered the bodies, a couple of them were covered in black soot. By the time they were finished handling the bodies, some of the people who had helped were also covered with black soot.

They thoroughly searched the plane and discovered only four officers on board. Upon reading the diary they had found lying close by, written by the pilot, First Lieutenant Grover C. Hodge, Jr., they learned that there were three other officers who had left by boat to try and find help.

After carefully removing the four bodies and securing them safely, the group slowly made its way back home to Hebron in the dark. The return trip took a little longer. Back home, the townspeople were all waiting to hear the results of their journey. In small communities like

Hebron, everyone knew what was going on, and they all shared each other's burdens.

The bodies were boarded on the plane and flown to St. John's. After their follow-up, the bodies were then returned to Chystal-l (Fort Chimo, now called Kuujjuaq) on April 22, 1943, where a funeral service was held, and interment took place in the United States cemetery plot the following day.

Acknowledgements

The site where this plane crashed has since become a radar site with a short paved runway. All that remains of this plane *Time's A Wastin'* is a heap of rust and the memories of those who lost their lives. May God grant them peace for the pain and suffering that they endured while the world, unfazed by their contribution, continued to live unaware of this formidable tragedy.

A special thank you to Christine Baikie, Larry Wilson. Scott Williams, and Jack Havener for their contributions to this book. Also, I would like to thank Flanker Press for agreeing to publish this important story. A special thanks to Ellis Coles for the lyrics to his song "Diary of One Now Dead."

A memorial to the ill-fated American crewmen of the B-26 Marauder *Time's A Wastin'* at the 5 Wing Goose Bay Museum. On display are the American flag and the Union Jack, and between them is the propeller of the doomed plane.

Appendix A
Diary of Pilot Hodge

The following is a copy of the diary that was written by the pilot, Grover Cleveland Hodge. It can be located in the 5 Wing Goose Bay Museum, Labrador.

NOV. 12, 1942 - We're still sitting here with 16 minutes of daylight each day. We've less than six hours of daylight between sunrise and sunset now. Had about two inches of snow last night and everything was really pretty. Spent most of the morning sweeping it off the plane. They said that there's a chance of leaving tomorrow but this place seems so much like home that it doesn't seem like we should leave.

NOV. 16, 1942 - This place is full of changes. Yesterday afternoon Jansen and I walked down to the river. There was a solid sheet of ice resting on the rocks, and it was covered with almost two inches of snow. Every once in a while, we would break through up to our knees, but there was nothing under the ice. Last night we had rain with a warm wind with gusts up to better than 60 miles per hour. So this morning there was only isolated patches of ice left. Today was the first time in two weeks that we have been able to walk on bare ground. We've had all kinds of weather, most of the days were fairly warm. But one day it was six degrees. We've seen days when not a breath of air stirred.

NOV. 26, 1942 - I still say this is screwy weather. We were alerted this morning at 0330. There was a solid overcast. We killed time until 0600 then we got briefed. It was still overcast and seemed to be getting worse. The A-10s and the B-25s started kicking off, but about then, it started to rain and the ceiling looked like it was very low. About ten minutes later it stopped raining and an A-20 came over at 600 feet with room to spare. By 0830, the sun was shining and everything looked as nice as we could ask for, but it was too late to take off.

DEC. 10, 1942 - Took off at last for Goose Bay. About 1315, we ran into some clouds and I turned around and called for the formation to turn around also. One plane dropped out. I think I saw the two P-40s later. I lost the others while letting down below the clouds. We saw an opening to the south at about 2,000 feet and after flying in that direction we broke out. We finally had to go back up to 13,000 feet, but it was clear sailing, so we kept on. Lt. Josephson gave me a new heading to get back on course, but we know now it was too much of a correction. About halfway I picked up Goose beam, but the set went dead after a few minutes. It was too late to turn back then, so we tried to get it on the compass, but couldn't. We finally hit the coast. We decided we were south of Goose Bay, so we turned north until we finally realized we were north. We were almost out of gas, so I started looking for a place to land. I wanted to get back where there were trees but the engines started missing, so we came back down, the crew never batted an eye when they were told that we were going to have to make a crash landing. Even if I do say so myself, it was a good landing and Lt. Josephson did a good job of cutting the switch, we hit a rock that tore the bomb bay open and one prop tip went through the fuselage behind me, outside of that the ship was intact. It swung around almost 90 degrees without stopping, but made a good wind break that way; it was almost dark so after eating a cold ration we went to bed inside of the ship; we had 17 blankets, a comforter and bed roll, but we slept very well. Lt. Josephson took a star shot and decided we were 300 minutes from Goose.

DEC. 11, 1942 - Lt. Josephson walked to the ford to the west and Golm the one to the east. We spent most of the day clearing up the ship and pooling rations in the afternoon. I climbed the mountain in front of us [where Saglek Air Station is now located], but didn't learn much. Nolan worked on the put-put all day without results. We cranked the dingy radio. It was pretty windy so we spent the night in the ship.

DEC. 12, 1942 - Made three big improvements in our situation. Lt. Jansen and Golm discovered a lake close to our ship and saw a fox. Weyrauch and I saw 50 seals; we know that there is food there. We made a lean-to out of tarps under the wing and slept out there. It was much better.

DEC. 13, 1942 - When the star shots were figured out it showed us to be close to the town of Hebron. Worked on the put-put all day with no success, so we tried to work the liaison set on the batteries but they were too weak. We pooled our covers and slept together.

DEC. 14, 1942 - Wind blew all day with increasing velocity and snow. Our lake went dry so we are back to melting snow. We went to bed early.

DEC. 15, 1942 - Had to eat a cold breakfast. Because the wind blew too much snow in our fire. Nolan changed the voltage regulators and got 25 volts, long enough for me to get a couple of stations on the liaison receiver. The put-put stopped, but we hope we know what is wrong with it. So we hope to get a message out soon.

DEC. 17, 1942 - The put-put out, but we did try the batteries. They, too, were dead.

DEC. 19, 1942 - More snow last night. Nolan and Mangini tried to work on the put-put but it was too cold. We built a fire in the lean-to and thawed out.

DEC. 20, 1942 - It was so windy we stayed in bed all day.

DEC. 21, 1942 - Everything was really snowed in so we spent the day eating and thawing out blankets and planning a trip south. Lt. Josephson, Lt. Jansen, and Sgt. Nolan plan to head south in the boat the first clear day.

DEC. 22, 1942 - Had a perfect day, the first clear day in over a week. We worked on the boat and cleaned snow away from the lean-to all day. We ate a pretty big meal with the three boat men eating a little extra.

DEC. 23, 1942 - Got up at 0715, got the boat ready and started carrying it. The wind was pretty strong and the boat was heavy, so we had a pretty hard time of it. We didn't get to the water until noon, and then it took quite a while to find a place to put it in the water. We intended to put them off shore, but they appeared to be making slow headway to the south. That was the last time we saw them. We had a hard time coming back against the snow. We had some peanuts and caramels and went to bed.

DEC. 24, 1942 - Christmas Eve and we've been here two weeks today. It was lonesome with just the four of us, but we got up pretty early and dug out the gas strainer so we could make a fire. It was so windy we couldn't work outside so we dried out the blankets. Golm got blistered pretty bad and swollen hands which had to be doctored. We stretched out our eating to cover most of the day. We had a sardine sized can of herring with crackers, a spoon full of peanuts apiece, a black cough drop, and a caramel, a cup of bouillon, a cup of grape drink, and plenty of coffee, using the same grounds over and over. It's really a surprise how much one can get from a small thing like a caramel, but we look forward to it with anticipation every day.

DEC. 25, 1942 - What a Christmas. Mangini's feet pained him so much we had to get up at 0330. He was in agony before that, but was better after. Although his arches pain him pretty bad. Got up again at 0900. Golm went exploring, I massaged Mangini's feet, and Weyrauch started fixing up the floor, which was in pretty bad condition from the fire. Later we had to dig out the rear entrance to the ship to fix the window up. After that, we had a first aid lesson. The only one who doesn't have anything wrong is me. We are about to eat our Christmas dinner and go to bed.

DEC. 26, 1942 - Had another swell day. The weather was perfect. Weyrauch cleaned up the back of the ship, while Golm dug around in the rear of the bomb bay, uncovering a can of fruit cocktail and a can of chicken a la king. I worked on Mangini's feet and did some odd jobs. Everyone is feeling better, and I hope that Mangini will be up in a few days. We aren't starving by any means, but the conversations are mostly about food. You surely can remember some good tasting food.

DEC. 27, 1942 - Started today as usual by treating the casualties. Mangini's feet are better, but we found a big blister on each foot. Golm and Mangini spent the day drying blankets. Weyrauch finished cleaning out the back of the ship, and I climbed the mountain to see if I could see anything out to sea. I also took a roll of film. The enforced diet is beginning to tell on us, but we eat at little more tomorrow.

DEC. 28, 1942 - This has been a terrible day. The wind started up early in the morning and has kept us inside all day. We had two fires which took the rest of the day to repair. Mangini's feet are quite a bit better, and he will start working on the put-put soon. We may get the liaison set going yet. In the meantime, we can feel the effects of the short rations more every day. We pray almost every minute that the boys in the boat will get through and get help soon.

DEC. 29, 1942 - Today has been just average. The wind started up early again, but not too hard. Mangini's feet are almost back to normal.

DEC. 30, 1942 - Today was overcast with snow showers. Spent most of the day working on the inside. Golm lost a finger nail, and may lose another. I'm just thankful that his hand doesn't pain him. Worked a little on the put-put and made some progress, but it was too dark to work much. Got up a game of 500 Rummy which everyone seemed to enjoy. The boys have been gone a week today. God grant that they are still going.

JAN. 1, 1943 - Happy New Year. It snowed and blew all night and kept it up all day. So since we had no fire we stayed in bed all day.

JAN. 2, 1943 - More wind and snow today. It slacked up a little around noon so we got up with the aid of a fire in a peanut can. Weyrauch got the prop and siphoned the tank out with a gallon of alcohol and glycerine, and I dug out the oil drain. After that, we had a couple of hot fires and plenty of coffee and had a lemon powder and a cup of bouillon. Our main dish was the last can of datenut roll with jelly, and it was very good. We didn't finish with the eating and drinking until almost noon. Then I worked on Mangini's feet, and we went to bed. There was quite a bit of loose snow outside but the very shape of the ship keeps it fairly clean. It actually rained today but I didn't know what effect that it's going to have on our situation. The boys have been gone ten days today, which is the time we figured it would take them to make the trip. We hope they made it and can bring help soon.

JAN. 3, 1943 - There wasn't much wind last night so we thought that we would have a good day, but the wind picked up, and it snowed all day. The ship has a sheet of ice on it and is covered with snow. Besides that, the drifts are higher and closer than they have ever been before. We hooked up the hand fuel transfer pump, and I'm positive we pumped some gas over to this side, but we couldn't get it to drain out, so we had to use the alcohol to cook with. I got into a big hurry once and caused a fire in which I got burned but not badly. Now we are all wearing bandages. I found two bouillon cubes in the radio operator's desk. Spent a lot of time putting snow under our bed. There was quite a hole there, so we should be able to sleep better tonight. It must be raining outside now. It couldn't be melting ice on the wing. We keep praying for clear weather and hope that the boys got through. Also to try out a new theory to where Hebron is.

JAN. 4, 1943 - Had a blue sky when we got up, but it stayed overcast all day. There wasn't much wind however, so we got up and went to work. Weyrauch and I got quite a bit of gas out of the other wing, so we are pretty well fixed on that. Mangini has the put-put almost ready to try again. We are just praying for good weather in hopes of a rescue plane (if the boys got through). I am cutting down still more on the rations.

JAN. 5, 1943 - It started off like a beautiful day, but turned to a light low overcast. Weyrauch and I cleaned the plane of snow and Mangini finished the put-put, which seems to be in pretty good shape. It started clearing late this afternoon.

JAN. 6, 1943 - This is the eighth day of bad weather. The entrance is blocked, and it doesn't do any good to dig it out. It has been two weeks since the boys have left and spirits are still high in spite of the bad weather.

JAN. 7, 1943 - We've been here four weeks today. The entrance was blocked up this morning. As I was going into the ship, I saw a little bird. We caught him and boiled him for a couple of hours. Then made stew by adding a bouillon powder. It was really delicious. Golm started to go looking for Hebron, but the snow was too soft. Mangini got outside for the first time in 13 days. If we can't find a town or get the put-put going in three days, we are going to have to sit and wait until the weather clears and pray that the boys got through because we are too low on food to do anything else. God help us get out of here safely.

JAN. 8, 1943 - Today was the most strenuous for me since we got here. I tried to get to Hebron, and I still think I know where it is, but there are two mountains in the way. I can feel myself growing weaker, and we have less to eat every day. I don't know what we would do if we didn't have that three pounds of coffee. We sit around and drink that and talk about all kinds of food, but I think we all crave chocolate candy more than anything else. The boys have dug out the back of the ship so if tomorrow is clear, we still have one last try with the put-put radio.

JAN. 9, 1943 - Well, we put the put-put back in its place, and it jammed again so that leaves us with one possibility, that the boys got through.

JAN. 10, 1943 - We have been here one month today, 31 days. Spent most of the day which was perfect as far as the weather was concerned looking for the plane and fixing up bandages. The boys' spirits were much higher today, after our little church service. Our only food today was a slice of pineapple and two spoonfuls of juice.

JAN. 11, 1943 - Our 3rd day of perfect weather, also the coldest day since right after we got here. Spent the day watching for the plane which didn't come. The oil gave out on this side, which brings about another problem. The short rations are beginning to tell on us, but we are still in high spirits. If we don't live to eat some of the food we talked about, we've ate [sic] mentally one of the best meals in the world.

119

JAN. 12, 1943 - Today was the boys' 20th day, our 33rd, and was overcast, but was calm. We got the oil almost dug out but are all so weak that we can hardly work. The boys' spirits are still high though, and we had a couple of lively bull sessions on our one topic, food. Our ration today was a slice of pineapple.

JAN. 13, 1943 - Another calm overcast day. We dug up the oil, dried out the blankets, made a new bed on snow, and ate our last food, a slice of spam and a soda cracker apiece. All we have left is a half of pound of chocolates and 3 drink powders, but we talk like rescue was certainly tomorrow. It cleared off late this afternoon, so maybe there is hope for tomorrow.

JAN. 14, 1943 - Clear day, but with wind. We cleared off the plane and waited, but nothing happened. Late this afternoon we were playing cards, Wren oiled the gas too fast and caused an explosion which burned both his and my face, hair, and hands. Our rations were 4 chocolates, but we are still working out pretty well. After a devotional, we went to bed.

JAN. 15, 1943 - A perfect day as to the weather, but the coldest since we got here. Spent most of the day trying to keep warm and listening for a plane. Also made big plans for a couple of days in New York when we get our furloughs. Rations were 2 chocolates and a bouillon powder. No one is particularly hungry yet, but we are getting weaker and colder because our bodies aren't putting out enough heat.

JAN. 16, 1943 - Another calm clear day, but the coldest we have yet had. The oil froze up, so we had to end up by burning nothing but gas. The only thing we have left is one bouillon powder and 2 sticks of gum. The strain is beginning to tell, but we still have good bull sessions about food and the furlough in New York.

JAN. 17, 1943 - Couldn't have asked for a better day except that it is so cold that the oil is frozen and won't burn. So our gas is going pretty fast. Had our last food, bouillon powder, so unless rescue comes in a few days, life will be over for us. The boys have been gone 25 days which is a long time, but they are still our only hope; our families will really miss some swell dishes and menus.

JAN. 18, 1943 - Cold and clear. My watch stopped, so we didn't get up until noon. Must be a little warmer because we got a little oil. Today was our first complete day without any food, but spirits are still pretty high. It's surprising how much punishment the body and mind can take when necessary. We are still in pretty good condition but rather weak. Not much hope left.

JAN. 20, 1943 - It snowed and blew all night, but we all slept pretty good and were much more cheerful today. We stayed longer than we should have though and are pretty tired. That snow has been blowing pretty hard all day and is piling up in front of the door, so I don't know what we will do if it doesn't stop pretty soon.

JAN. 21, 1943 - Six weeks today and rough night with snow and rain, so everything was soaked when we got up. Only Weyrauch and I got up and then only long enough to melt snow for water. Things could be worse.

JAN. 22, 1943 - Got up around noon, and was up until about 6. I cleared up the entrance and made the bed. We could stand some good weather.

JAN. 23, 1943 - Spent a miserable night. Everyone got crowded and nobody could get comfortable. Had a good day, but everybody is pretty discouraged, although the conversation was pretty good. We haven't really felt famished, but we are really weak. It really gets me to see these boys start to do something and have to stop from lack of power to go on. Weyrauch has developed a case of piles and is really suffering.

JAN. 24, 1943 - Had a miserable night. Everybody got up at one thirty, shot the bull and drew gas, and went to bed at seven thirty.

JAN. 25, 1913 - Cold night, clear day, but still pretty bad.

JAN. 26, 1943 - Overcast but fairly calm. Each day we don't see how we can last another day, but each time we manage to go on. We all smoked a pipe of tobacco this morning and Golm really got sick, and I felt pretty bad. But we came out pretty well.

FEB. 3, 1943 - Slept a solid week in bed. Today Weyrauch died after being mentally ill for several days. We are all pretty weak, but should be able to last several more days.

* * * * *

This is a list of the food that was on the plane when they landed. It was the only food that they had to live off for the last months of their lives.

7 cans of Spam
3 cans of peanuts
8 cans of chicken
3 cans of fruit cocktail
2 cans of date nut roll
1 can of brown bread
3 boxes of chocolate
28 Hershey bars
4 packages of dates
1 pound of crackers

4 boxes of fig newtons
1 pound of cheese crackers
1 case of Coke
2 cans of salmon
3 pounds of coffee
20 packages of caramels

Appendix B
1972 Andes Flight Disaster
(A Comparative Story)

On October 13, 1972, a Uruguayan Air Force twin turbo-prop Fairchild FH-227D was on a chartered flight carrying a rugby team, their friends, and associates. It crashed in the remote mountains in Argentina, near the border of Chile. Of the twenty-nine passengers who survived, eight more were killed a few days later by an avalanche that swept over their shelter in the wreckage.

Uruguayan air force crash of Fairchild FH-227D, on
October 13, 1972

The remaining survivors had very little food and no source of heat at an altitude of 11,800 feet. They were facing starvation. According to radio news reports, the search for them was called off after some efforts were made. Survivors then had no other choice, after their food ran out, but to resort to cannibalism. One lady refused to partake, because of her beliefs. She died shortly after.

Rescuers did not learn of the survivors until seventy-two days after the crash, when a couple of passengers, after a ten-day trek across the Andes, found Chilean Arriero Sergio Catalan, who gave them food and then alerted authorities about the other survivors.

They had crashed only about eighteen miles west of an abandoned hotel. Several brief expeditions were made in the immediate vicinity of the plane in the first few weeks after the crash, but they found that a combination of altitude sickness, dehydration, snow blindness, malnourishment, and the extreme cold of the nights made climbing any significant distance an impossible task.

Appendix C
"Diary of One Now Dead"
by Ellis Coles

He throttled her up at Greenland,
Quickly towards heaven she did soar,
That Yankee B-26, en route to Goose Bay, Labrador,
Not knowing it would be the last time
They would fly together in the blue,
And that Saglek would be the fate
For that bomber and her crew.

By the thirtieth of November,
It was in the year of forty-two,
She struck a storm of heavy cloud,
And right away that Yankee pilot knew,
To navigate the winter storm far up north
Sometimes the chips are down,

So he altered course and flew due south,
Saying, "Boys, we'll have to go around."

Many miles later, far out to sea,
He turned that bird around,
Josephson he set a course,
Once more for Goose Bay they were bound;
They made contact with Goose Bay
Just minutes before the radio went dead,
"We'll have to fly by compass now,"
The navigator to that pilot said.

They struck the coast of Labrador,
Just where there seemed to be some doubt,
They flew due north 'cause somehow figured
They were flying too far south;
But they figured wrong 'cause some miles later,
Farther down that coast they somehow found,
They were flying too far north,
And once again they turned that bird around.

Then the engine started missin',
As the gauges read completely out of fuel,
"Find a valley quickly,
We must take her down,
That's all there's left to do."
Well, she crashed between the mountains,
Came to rest among great boulders still intact;

Guess her last flight had ended,
Among the barren hills of Saglek.

In the crash just badly shaken,
With minor cuts, but everyone all right,
They ate up some full rations,
And prepared to lie down for the night;
Then Josephson he stepped outside,
When he saw that star his sexton came in use,
And soon it was decided,
He was four hundred miles north of Goose.

From that same star decided that,
The little town of Hebron was nearby,
But they never tried to reach it,
I guess we'll always have to wonder why;
But they stayed inside and waited,
While being cold and hungry all in vain,
Waitin' for the sound of the engine
Of the plane that never came.

Just you fancy livin' in
The belly of a plane, forty below,
And every morn waking with
Your blankets cold, frozen,
White with snow;
With not a stick of wood,
Just the rocky barren hills of a frozen land,

And your only source of heat
Was the heat of burning gas in old tin cans.

One day they came upon a plan,
A plan they thought would work without a doubt,
Jansen, Golm and Josephson
Would take a rubber boat and row south;
Two days before Christmas,
They dropped that rubber boat into the bay,
"We'll send back help when we arrive,"
Said goodbye
And slowly rowed away.

Now, men will always gamble,
With women, cards and money evermore,
But no man there to gamble in,
An open boat off Northern Labrador;
Out of total desperation they gambled
With their lives and hoped to win,
But the odds were stacked against them,
These three brave men were never seen again.

And back in Saglek,
In the belly of the plane, life went on,
Gettin' weaker, weather colder,
Soon December month had passed and gone;
And January only brought more days
Of cold, hunger and despair,

Their spirits low, their hopes were gone,
The will to live no longer there.

In the first month on the seventeenth,
They shared a cup of soup—their very last,
Their food all gone, and not too strong,
They knew right then that life was slipping fast;
For days they lay in slumber,
Just bundled there together near the end,
And on the third day, second month,
He wrote into his diary once again:

"We're growin' weak and tired,
But we pray to God we last a few more days,
But our hopes are gettin' weaker,
We just saw young Weyrauch slip away."
These were the last words written,
And in my mind they help to take us back,
To the night that Jesus called them home,
From that frozen hell called Saglek.

'Twas early in the month of March,
Several Eskimos on dog and sleigh,
Went down between the mountains
To hunt for fur and food
In St. John's Bay;
Early in their journey,
Barely thirty miles they had gone,

When they found four frozen bodies
Just three and one-half hours from Hebron.

Now this story is not fiction,
To bring the facts to you I've really tried,
'Cause I'm here now in Saglek
The very spot where these men crashed and died;
And in my hand I'm holdin',
The diary that many times I've read,
I guess the cover says it all:
The Diary of One Now Dead.

Recorded by Ellis Coles (*All the Best*, 1995)

Appendix D
"Historic Marauder Firsts"
by Jack Havener

Historic "firsts" add significant accomplishments of the Martin B-26 Marauder that placed it will ahead of its time and proved it to be the premier USAAF bomber of World War II, a recognition it never received during the war.

1. It was the first combat aircraft to use butted seam skin covering instead of overlapping. This reduced drag.

2. It had the first aerodynamically perfect fuselage. An early nickname was "Flying Torpedo."

3. It was the first combat aircraft to use plastics as metal substitutes on a grand scale, over 400 parts.

4. It was the first WWII vintage bomber to use a four-bladed propeller: Curtiss-Electric.

5. It had the first horizontal tail plans with a marked dihedral: eight degrees.

6. The first model off the production line was the prototype—and it flew! The Army Air Corps was so anxious to get the revolutionary high-speed bomber that it didn't allow for the usual prototype models for testing.

7. It was the first twin-engine bomber to carry more payload of bombs than the B-17 of the time: 4,000 pounds.

8. It was the first American WWII bomber to carry a power-operated gun turret. Built by Martin and used on many other US bombers, and also the British Lancaster.

9. It was the first US combat aircraft with self-sealing fuel tanks as regular equipment. Developed by Martin in 1936, manufactured by US Rubber Co., and called Mareng cells.

10. It had the first all-Plexiglas bombardier's nose.

11. It was the first to use flexible tracks for transferring ammunition from storage boxes in the waist section to the tail guns. These were made by Lionel Trains.

12. It was the first medium bomber in which the tail gunner could sit upright.

13. It was the first combat bomber to employ an all-electrical bomb release system.

14. It comprised the first Air Force bombardment group to leave the USA for a combat zone in WWII. The 22nd Bomb Group left Langley Field, Virginia, for the west coast on December 8 and flew coastal defence duty for a time. On February 6, 1942, it left San Francisco by ship to Hawaii. At Hickam Field the planes were reassembled and flown to Australia.

15. The 22nd was also the first completely armed air force group to fly the Pacific (Hawaii to Australia) in full.

16. The B-26 was used by more air forces in WWII then any other US combat aircraft: US Army Air Force, US Navy, US Marine Corps, British RAF Balkan Air Force, British RAF South African Air Force, and the Free French Air Force.

17. The B-26s of the 69th and 70th Squadrons of the 38th Bomb Group were the first twin-engine bomber outfits to fly from California to Hawaii. They were on their way to the South Pacific to join the 22nd Bomb Group. It was never done thereafter doing WWII.

18. It was the first US medium bomber to fly combat in the South Pacific: 22nd Bomb Group on April 5, 1942.

19. It was the first army bomber to use torpedoes against a Japanese fleet in the South Pacific: in early June 1942 at the Battle of Midway.

20. A few days later, it was the first army bomber to launch torpedoes against a Japanese task force in the Aleutians, which was trying to maintain a foothold on the islands of Attu and Kiska. This was the first and only time during WWII that an enemy force occupied US territory.

21. The B-26 was the first WWII American aircraft to use weapons pods: two on either side of the forward fuselage carrying .50-calibre machine guns firing forward and operated by a button on the pilot's control wheel.

22. In November 1943, the first Marauder built was finally retired to the Ford Dearborn Engine school for instructional purposes. Ford built the Pratt A. Whitney R-20W engine for Martin and the B-26. "Old Gran Pappy" was the first bomber of any type to still be on active service. It was used for training purposes at many airfields and finally at Laughlin Army Air Field, Del Rio, Texas, where it set an endurance record for training planes by hauling more than 100 pilots on flights, teaching them to fly the B-26, for a total of 2,180 hours without a serious mishap or casualty of any kind.

23. The first ever B-26 to complete fifty combat missions was *Hell Cat*, a B-26 B2 of the 17th Bomb Group. The event occurred in late spring 1943, when the group was stationed at Djedaida, Tunisia. Subsequently, *Hell Cat* and her crew, including the crew chief, were sent back to the United States to participate in war bond tours. Today, one of the 1/72 scale plastic model kits of the B-26 is *Hell Cat.*

24. The 319th Bomb Group became the first outfit of any USAAF aircraft type to try six-abreast takeoffs and landings in North Africa to save time and fuel. The dust created became a hazard, so it was discontinued until the group was based at Decimomannu Airfield in Sardinia, where a 1,200-foot-wide harder surface runway was available with oiled-down takeoff lanes.

25. The 17th Bomb Group, the "daddy of them all," racked up more total combat missions (606) during its tour in the Mediterranean theatre of operations than any other Marauder group in WWII. Its last mission was flown on May 1, 1945, and not only did it fly one that day, but it went out in a blaze of glory by flying two.

26. The B-26 was the first medium bomber modified for tow target use in aerial gunnery training with pursuit plane speed. It was designated AT-23 but was later changed to TB-26.

27. The first Allied bomber in the Mediterranean theatre of operations to complete 100 combat missions was B-2E *Hells Bells II* on May 1, 1944.

28. The first Allied bomber in the European theatre of operations to complete 100 combat missions was B-26 *Mild and Bitter* on May 9, 1944.

29. The proudest accomplishment of the Martin Marauder came on D-Day, June 8, 1944, when it was chosen by General Eisenhower to spearhead Operation Overlord, the invasion of Normandy. Eight 9th Air Force groups of B-26s led the entire Allied bomber stream and bombed shore installations at Utah and Omaha Beaches just minutes ahead of the troop landings.

30. The B-26 was the first Allied bomber in the European theatre of operations to complete 200 combat missions. This was accomplished on April 17, 1945, and the forward section of *Flak Bait* now resides in the Air and Space Museum of the Smithsonian in Washington, DC.

31. The B-26 had the lowest combat loss rate of any US aircraft: less than one half of one per cent.

32. The only B-26H (which was actually a G model retrofitted) became the first aircraft to test a bicycle-type landing gear, as would later be incorporated with the B-47 and B-52 jet bombers. This took place at the Glenn L. Martin Company's Middle River, Maryland, factory in October 1945.

33. It was the only combat aircraft of WWII that the Air Force dictated that all that survived the war be scrapped. Those left in the South Pacific ware scrapped in Australia, all those left in the European theatre of war were scrapped in Germany, and those in the Aleutians that had been replaced by the B-25 in 1943 were flown back to the United States to join all those in the US scrapped out in a huge reclamation facility at Walnut Ridge, Arkansas. Fortunately, a few still exist. The only one in flying condition belongs to the Kermit Weeks Fantasy of Flight Museum in Polk City, Florida. It was salvaged from a wreck of three that force landed in Canada on their way to Alaska. They were all the B-26 "straight"—the first ones built. The other two hulks are painstakingly being restored to static display condition at the MAPS Museum in Canton, Ohio, and the Beaver Falls Museum in Pennsylvania. *Flak Bait* (at least part of it) is on static display in the Smithsonian, and a G model is on static display at the Air Force Museum in Dayton, Ohio. This airplane was traded to the museum by the French Air Force, which was using it for mechanical instructional purposes, for a C-47. The only other one left is being restored at the Paris Air Museum, and it was the other G model that the French Air Force, and later Air France, used for mechanical instructional purposes.

Appendix E
Ten Worst Air Crashes and Disasters of All Time

The following is a list of the worst air crashes and disasters of all time, followed by other major disasters.

History has witnessed many aviation accidents, and many of those air crashes were fatal, in which many people died and were injured. Many times these accidents were due to mechanical error, and many of them were due to human error. To avoid these accidents, air safety has been improved over a hundred years. To provide safety landing gears, turbine engines and evacuation slides have been introduced.

Pan American World Airways 103 (1988)

On December 21, 1988, the Pam Am was blasted to pieces. It broke in two main sections and crashed in Lockerbie. The explosive device was planted in the cargo area by terrorists. There were 243 passengers aboard and sixteen crew members. All of the passengers and crew members died, along with eleven citizens of Lockerbie. In total, there were 270 fatalities.

Islamic Revolutionary Guard Corps Plane Crash

Both the engines of the plane failed in this crash. Ten elite officers of Iranian Revolutionary Guards died, including the commander. There were a total of 275 passengers and crew members who died. Poor weather conditions were the cause of this crash. It crashed into an 11,500-foot-high hill.

A Falcon jet belonging to the Iranian Revolutionary Guards Corps crashed January 9, 2006.

Iran Air 655 (1988)

While this aircraft was flying over the Persian Gulf (Iran's territorial seas), a Cruiser-A United States guided Navy missile blew the plane apart. All 290 passengers were killed. According to the US government, they thought that it was a Tomcat Fighter. The US government did not apologize but gave a compensation of $61.8 million.

A300B2-203 Iran Air EP-IBT

Saudi Arabia Airlines 163 (1980)

This flight took off from Riyadh International Airport. After seven minutes, the plane caught fire. The flight attendants got a warning, and a lot of crucial time was wasted confirming it. The captain realized he should return to the airport, and he did so. Due to fire, engine #2 was shut down, and the pilot declared an emergency landing. The pilot continued to a taxi way. He should have ordered an emergency evacuation, but he did not. As a result of the smoke, all 301 passengers died.

Lockheed L-1011 Tristar

Air India 182 (1985)

The plane was known as *Emperor Kanishka*. It was blown up by a bomb and crashed in the Atlantic Ocean. The aircraft was travelling on a Montreal–London–Delhi route. The total number of people killed was 329. Most officials blamed Sikh extremists for this crash. 268 Canadians died aboard the flight.

Boeing 747-200 (VT-EFO, Emperor Kanishka).

Turkish Airlines 981 (1974)

Turkish Airlines 981 crashed in Oise, France, as a result of a failed cargo hatch latching system. The hatch blew in the flight, the cabin floors collapsed, and the control cables were damaged, taking the flight out of the air. All 346 passengers were killed.

Saudi Arabia Airlines (1996)

A mid-air collision occurred in 1996 above New Delhi. Neither of the planes were using any airborne collision avoidance system. Due to some kind of misunderstanding and confusion, the pilot of IL76 believed the flight was clear to continue down, but both the aircraft were on the same route. All 349 passengers were killed.

McDonnell DouglasDC-10-10, Turkish Airlines AN1815013

Boeing 747-168B, Saudi Arabia Airlines AN0217717

Japan Airlines (1985)

The Japan Airlines plane crashed due to a mechanical problem. It crashed 100 kilometres away from Tokyo. There were only four survivors and 520 deaths. The rear bulkhead resulted in explosive decompression, which damaged all four hydraulic systems. There was also lack of oxygen. The aircraft began to oscillate and crashed. Delayed rescue operation also contributed to some of the deaths.

Boeing 747SR-46, Japan Airlines JA8119

Pan American Airways (1977)

The Pan Am flight was called off due to a bomb explosion. The KLM flight was also called off for same reason. The crew replaced and locked off the thrust reverser of engine #3. Witnesses described an explosion due to a missile, but no criminal attack was detected. There were 644 total passengers and crew and 583 fatalities.

KLM Boeing 747-206B (PH-BUF) named The Rhine.

American Airlines (2001)

This plane was hijacked when it took off from Logan International Airport. 260 people in the plane died, and five people on the ground were killed. It was one of the four planes hijacked the same day. It crashed into the World Trade Center between 96th and 99th floors. The whole building collapsed after some time.

Airbus A300B4-605R, American Airlines N14053

Appendix F
Other Major Disasters

Air France Flight 447

Air France Flight 447 (abbreviated AF447) was a scheduled international flight from Galeão International Airport in Rio de Janeiro, Brazil, to Charles de Gaulle International Airport in Paris, France. On June 1, 2009, the Airbus A330-203 airliner serving the flight crashed into the Atlantic Ocean, resulting in the deaths of all 216 passengers and twelve aircrew. The accident was the deadliest in the history of Air France. It was also the Airbus A330's second and deadliest fatal accident, and its first while in commercial passenger service.

While Brazilian authorities were able to locate the first major wreckage within five days of the accident, initial investigation was hampered because the aircraft's black boxes were not recovered from the ocean floor until May 2011, nearly two years later. The final report, released at a news conference on July 5, 2012, stated that the aircraft crashed after temporary inconsistencies between the airspeed measurements—likely due to the aircraft's pitot tubes being obstructed by ice crystals—caused the autopilot to disconnect, after which the crew reacted incorrectly and ultimately led the aircraft to an aerodynamic stall from which they did not recover.

September 11 Attacks

The deadliest aviation-related disaster of any kind, considering fatalities on both the aircraft and the ground, was the destruction of the World Trade Center in New York City on September 11, 2001. On that morning, four aircraft travelling from east coast airports to California were hijacked by nineteen terrorists affiliated with Al Qaeda, with the intentional crashing of American Airlines Flight 11 and United Airlines Flight 175 into the Twin Towers of the World Trade Center, destroying both buildings in less than two hours. The World Trade Center crashes killed 2,752, the vast majority of them occupants of the World Trade Center towers or emergency personnel responding to the disaster. In addition, 184 were killed by American Airlines Flight 77, which crashed into the Pentagon, causing severe damage to the building's west side, and forty were killed when United Airlines Flight 93 crashed into a Pennsylvania field (after passengers fought back against the hijackers). This brought the total number of casualties of the September 11 attacks to 2,977 (excluding the nineteen terrorist hijackers).

As deliberate terrorist acts, the 9/11 crashes were not classified as accidents, but as mass murder–suicide. This event was subsequently treated by the United States and the member states of NATO as an act of war and terrorism.

Tenerife

The Tenerife disaster, which happened on March 27, 1977, remains the accident with the highest number of airliner passenger fatalities. 583 people died when a KLM Boeing 747 attempted to take off without clearance and collided with a taxiing Pan Am 747 at Los Rodeos Airport on the island of Tenerife, Spain. Both aircraft were destroyed. There were no survivors from the KLM aircraft; 61 of the 396 passengers and crew on the Pan Am aircraft survived. Pilot error was the primary cause, as the KLM captain thought he had clearance for takeoff due to a communication misunderstanding. A contributing factor was dense fog: the KLM flight crew was unable to see the Pan Am aircraft on the runway until immediately prior to the collision. The accident had a lasting influence on the industry, particularly in the area of communication. An increased emphasis was placed on using standardized phraseology in ATC communication by both controllers and pilots alike, thereby reducing the chance for misunderstandings. As part of these changes, the word "takeoff" was removed from general usage and is only spoken by ATC when actually clearing an aircraft to take off.

JAL Flight 123

The crash of Japan Airlines Flight 123, on August 12, 1985, is the single-aircraft disaster with the highest number of fatalities: 520 died on board the Boeing 747. The aircraft suffered an explosive decompression from an incorrectly repaired aft pressure bulkhead, which failed in mid-flight, destroying most of its vertical stabilizer, severing all of the hydraulic lines, and making the 747 virtually uncontrollable. Pilots were able to keep the plane flying for twenty minutes after departure before crashing into a mountain. Remarkably, several people survived, but by the time the Japanese rescue teams arrived at the crash site, all but four had succumbed to their injuries.

Other Crashes with High Death Tolls

November 12, 2001

American Airlines Flight 587, an Airbus A300, crashed in the Belle Harbor neighbourhood of Queens, New York, just after departing John F. Kennedy International Airport bound for Las Américas International Airport, Santo Domingo. The first officer's overuse of the rudder in response to wake turbulence from a Japan Airlines 747 was cited as the cause. The crash killed all 260 people on board, as well as five people on the ground. It is the second-deadliest aviation accident on US soil, after American Airlines Flight 191.

July 25, 2000

Air France Flight 4590—a Concorde—crashed, resulting in the death of 109 people on board as well as four on the ground. Although Concorde jets had a very good safety record with no previous crashes, this event was the beginning of the end for the aircraft; the high-prestige supersonic plane was retired from service by both British Airways and Air France in 2003. The official finding traced the cause of a fuel tank rupture to the plane's impact with an aircraft part on the runway that had fallen off a previously departed airliner. According to the documentary *Counterfeit Culture*, the crash in part was due to the use of a counterfeit component on that aircraft.

October 31, 1999

Around 01:50 EST, in international waters, Egypt Air Flight 990 (MSR990) crashed into the Atlantic Ocean, about sixty miles south of Nantucket Island, Massachusetts, killing all 217 people on board. The National Transportation Safety Board report concluded the first officer intentionally drove the aircraft into the ocean; Egyptian authorities have vigorously denied this conclusion, saying a mechanical failure was to blame.

September 2, 1998

Swissair Flight 111 crashed into St. Margaret's Bay, near Halifax, Nova Scotia, killing all 229 people on board. Fire had broken out in the cockpit; the plane disintegrated upon impact with the water.

November 12, 1996

The world's deadliest mid-air collision was the 1996 Charkhi Dadri mid-air collision involving Saudia Flight 763 and Air Kazakhstan Flight 1907 over Haryana, India. The crash was mainly the result of the Kazakh pilot flying lower than the assigned clearance altitude. All 349 passengers and crew on board the two aircraft died. The Ramesh Chandra Lahoti Commission, empowered to study the causes, recommended the creation of "air corridors" to prevent aircraft from flying in opposite directions at the same altitude. The Civil Aviation Authorities in India made it mandatory for all aircraft flying in and out of India to be equipped with a TCAS (traffic collision avoidance system), setting a worldwide precedent for mandatory use.

July 17, 1996

TWA Flight 800 exploded and crashed into the Atlantic Ocean near East Moriches, New York, twelve minutes after takeoff from John F. Kennedy International Airport, killing all 230 people on board.

May 26, 1991

Shortly after takeoff from Bangkok, Lauda Air Flight 004, a Boeing 767-3Z9ER named *Wolfgang Amadeus Mozart*, crashed in Thailand. The uncommanded deployment of one of the thrust reversers caused the loss of all 223 passengers and crew aboard the 767.

December 21, 1988

Pan Am Flight 103, a Boeing 747-121 bound for New York-JFK from London-Heathrow with continued service to Detroit was destroyed by a terrorist bomb over the town of Lockerbie, Scotland. The crash killed all 243 passengers and sixteen crew, and eleven people on the ground (all residents of Sherwood Crescent, Lockerbie), making it the worst terrorist attack involving an aircraft in the UK. This remains the deadliest terrorist attack on British soil. Following the crash, the Federal Aviation Administration imposed new security measures on American airlines flying out of 103 airports in Western Europe and the Middle East.

July 3, 1988

Iran Air Flight 655 was an Iranian civilian airliner shot down by two surface-to-air missiles from the US Navy's guided missile cruiser USS *Vincennes* over the Strait of Hormuz, killing all 290 passengers and crew aboard, ranking it seventh among the deadliest airline disasters.

August 16, 1987

Northwest Airlines Flight 255, a Northwest Airlines Mc-Donnell Douglas MD-82 with six crew members and 149 passengers, en route to Phoenix, stalled shortly after takeoff from Detroit-Wayne County Metropolitan Airport with the engines at takeoff power, but the wing flaps and slats were not properly set. All occupants but one, as well as two motorists on Middlebelt Road, perished.

June 23, 1985

Air India Flight 182, a Boeing 747-237B, crashed off the southwest coast of Ireland when a bomb exploded in the cargo hold. All 307 passengers and twenty-two crew members died. One passenger had checked in as "M. Singh." Singh did not board the flight, but his suitcase containing the bomb was loaded onto the plane. Singh was never identified and captured. It was later determined Sikh extremists were behind the bombing as a retaliation for the Indian government's attack on the Golden Temple in the city of Amritsar. This was, at the time, the deadliest terrorist attack involving an airplane.

December 12, 1985

A Douglas DC-8, Arrow Air Flight 1285, carrying American military personnel on a charter flight home for Christmas, crashed in Newfoundland, killing all 248 passengers and eight crew members. The Canadian Aviation Safety Board investigating the cause of the crash issued two different reports: the majority report cited ice on the wings as the cause of the crash; the minority report suggests an explosion was the likely cause. This crash remains the worst air disaster in both US military and Canadian aviation history.

September 1, 1983
A Soviet interceptor Sukhoi Su-15 shot down Korean Air Lines Flight 007, a Boeing 747-230B, after it flew into Soviet airspace, killing all 269 passengers and crew.

May 25, 1979
American Airlines Flight 191, a McDonnell Douglas DC-10-10, following improper maintenance and the loss of an engine, lost control and crashed near O'Hare International Airport in Des Plaines, Illinois. The crash killed all 271 passengers and crew on board, as well as two people on the ground. It remains the deadliest commercial aircraft accident in United States history and was also the country's deadliest aviation disaster until the September 11 attacks in 2001.

March 3, 1974
Turkish Airlines Flight 981, a McDonnell Douglas DC-10, crashed in a forest northeast of Paris, France. The London-bound plane crashed shortly after taking off from Orly Airport; all 346 people on board died. It was later determined that the cargo door detached, which caused an explosive decompression; this caused the floor just above to collapse. The collapsed floor severed the control cables, which left the pilots without control of the elevators, the rudder, and #2 engine. The plane entered a steep dive and crashed. It was the deadliest plane crash of all time until the Tenerife disaster in 1977.

Appendix G
Investigation Report

The documents on the following pages are copies from the investigation report conducted by the United States Air Armed Forces.

P.O. #858 C/o Postmaster,
New York, N.Y. —

1526 Z,   43-12-10-50(

Lt. Hodge was the leader of a flight of B-26's. The flight had to fly at about 11,500 ft. due to clouds. Two wing men were lost from Lt. Hodge's sight & he ordered them to return to their base.

The last seen of Lt. Hodge was at about 13,000 ft. circling in a clear area.

It is believed Lt. Hodge encountered weather or mechanical difficulties beyond his status of training or performance of his aircraft

J.B. H.

WAR DEPARTMENT
A.A.F. Form No. 14
(Revised May 15, 1942)

ACCIDENT No. **60**

WAR DEPARTMENT
U. S. ARMY AIR FORCES
REPORT OF AIRCRAFT ACCIDENT

(1) Place **APO #658, c/o Postmaster, New York, N.Y.** Date **December 10, 1942** (3) Time **1935 Z**
AIRCRAFT: (4) Type and model **B-26** (5) A. F. No. **41-17862** (6) Station **In transit.**
Organization: (7) **3rd A.F.** (8) **319th Bomb.** (9) **440th Bomb.**
(Command and Air Force) (Group) (Squadron)

PERSONNEL

Duty (10)	NAME (Last name first) (11)	Rating (12)	Serial No. (13)	Rank (14)	Personnel Class (15)	Branch (16)	Air Force or Command (17)	Result to Personnel (18)	Use of Parachute (19)
P	Hodge, Grover C.	P	O-789226	1st Lt.	201	A.C.	3rd A.F.	Lost	Unknown
CP	Jansson, Paul M.	P	O-727861	2nd Lt.	2030	"	"	"	"
N	Josephson, Emanuel J.	N	O-727019	2nd Lt.	2018	"	"	"	"
B	Gale, Frank J.	B	12037633	Cpl.	1812	"	"	"	"
E	Weyranch, Russell (MM)	G	16042586	Sgt.	1812	"	"	"	"
G	Mangini, James J., Jr.	G	12077708	Cpl.	1812	"	"	"	"
I	Nolen, Charles F.	R	32174825	Sgt.	1812	"	"	"	"

PILOT CHARGED WITH ACCIDENT

(20) **Hodge** **George** **C.** (21) O-789226 (22) **Lt.** (23) **201** (24) **A.C.**
(Last name) (First name) (Middle initial) (Serial number) (Rank) (Personnel class) (Branch)

Assigned (25) **3rd A.F.** (26) **319th Bomb.** (27) **440th Bomb.** (28) **In transit.**
(Command and Air Force) (Group) (Squadron) (Station)

Attached for flying (29) (30) (31) (32)
(Command and Air Force) (Group) (Squadron) (Station)

Original rating (33) **P** (34) **4-29-42** Present rating (35) **P** (36) **4-29-42** Instrument rating (37) **7-20-42**
(Rating) (Date) (Rating) (Date) (Date)

First Pilot Hours: **No record at this station.**
(at the time of this accident)
(38) This type **Approximately** 375:00 (42) Instrument time last 6 months **Approx.** 11:00
(39) This model " 300:00 (43) Instrument time last 30 days 1:00
(40) Last 90 days " 50:00 (44) Night time last 6 months 100:00
(41) Total " 700:00 (45) Night time last 30 days 0:00

AIRCRAFT DAMAGE

DAMAGE (49) LIST OF DAMAGED PARTS

(46) Aircraft **Complete loss.**
(47) Engine(s)
(48) Propeller(s)

(50) Weather at the time of accident **See route forecast folder.**

(51) Was the pilot flying on instruments at the time of accident **Unknown.**
(52) Cleared from **Oncto** (53) To **Alkali** (54) Kind of clearance **Contact or on top**
of broken clouds.
(55) Pilot's mission **Ferrying aircraft to PLAAF for rerouting by way of South Atlantic**

(56) Nature of accident **Undetermined.**

(57) Cause of accident **Undetermined.**

DESCRIPTION OF ACCIDENT

(Brief narrative of accident. Include statement of responsibility and recommendations for action to prevent repetition)

On 12-10-42 Omoto and Goose giving, and forecasting to remain, favorable weather with weather forecasted as good it was decided to clear B-26's to Goose. Tops were forecasted to be about 13,000 feet and the pilots were cautioned against instrument flying.

Lt. Hodge's flight departed O*oto at 1257 G.M.T. and formed west of Sancho.

About 250 miles west of the Greenland Coast the flight encountered thin high clouds. Lt. Hodge led his flight into openings and breaks at 8,000 feet and started climbing. As the clouds thickened Lt. Hodge ordered a 180 degree turn but lost two of his wing men in the clouds. Lt. Hodge then ordered the two ships to return. Lt. Peppin, right wing man, radioed back that he was in the clear at 11,500 feet and was told to proceed to Goose. Another wing man, Lt. Gammon, was having radio trouble and at no time heard Lt. Hodge; he topped everything at 13,000 feet and proceeded to Goose. The third wing man, Lt. Floyd, followed Lt. Hodge.

Lt. Hodge, followed by Lt. Floyd, circled in a clear area at 13,000 feet, Lt. Floyd was circling with frozen controls when he saw the lead ship head in the general direction of Goose. This was the last seen of Lt. Hodge.

Unable to follow, Lt. Floyd, when his controls freed, returned to Omoto;

It is believed Lt. Hodge encountered weather or mechanical difficulties beyond his status of training and the performance of his aircraft and this was directly responsible for the loss of his aircraft.

See attached reports made by other pilots cleared west that morning and the route forecast folder turned in by an R.A.F.F.C. eastbound pilot.

Signature EARL W. SWEENEY, Lt. Col., A.C.
DANIEL E. LINDSEY, Capt., A.C.
ROBERT E. GRIFFIN, Capt., A.C.

Date 12-13-42

APO #858, c/o Postmaster,
New York, New York.

December 10, 1942

I was flying on Lt Hodges left wing when we encountered this high clouds. This was approximately 1445 GMT and about 200 to 250 miles from the coast of Greenland. We entered the clouds at about 7000 ft and began to pick our way through the openings and the thinest portions of the clouds and at the same time gaining altitude. The clouds were very thin and Lt Hodge was in sight most of the time. I picked up a little wing ice in these clouds.

The last time I saw Lt Hodge was a couple minutes before I broke out of this cloud bank. We were at ten thousand ft. and Lt Hodge made a slight turn to the left and crossed over the top of us. I broke out of the bank and was over the top of the overcast at 13000. Lt hodge did not come out of the clouds so I continued to Goose Bay. There were two other planes in our formation when we started picking our way through the clouds. I lost the other two planes the same time I ost sight of Lt Hodge.

At no time did I hear Lt Hodge on the radio although at the time I was having trouble with my radio.

The overcast was solid until we reached the coast after that there were scattered clouds. The top was 12000 lowering to 9000 at the coast.

A TRUE COPY:

ROBERT E. GRIFFIN,
Captain, Air Corps,
Control Officer.

Signed   ALBERT L. GAMMON
1st Lt AAF
440th Bomb Sq.

WAR DEPARTMENT
A.A.F. Form No. 14
(Revised May 15, 1942)

SUPPLEMENTAL REPORT

WAR DEPARTMENT

U. S. ARMY AIR FORCES

REPORT OF AIRCRAFT ACCIDENT

Accident No. 43-12-10-501

(1) Place North Bank of Cape Suglek, Labrador (2) Date December 10, 1942 (3) Time 1855 GMT

AIRCRAFT: (4) Type and model B-26B (5) A. F. No. 41-17862 (6) Station in transit

Organization: (7) Air Transport (Command and Air Force) (8) 319th Bomb. (Group) (9) 440th Bombardment (Squadron)

PERSONNEL

Duty (10)	NAME (Last name first) (11)	Rating (12)	Serial No. (13)	Rank (14)	Personnel Class (15)	Branch (16)	Air Force or Command (17)	Result to Personnel (18)	Use of Parachute (19)
P	Hodge, Grover C.	P	O-789226	1st Lt	18	A.C.	A.T.C.	Fatal	None
CP	Jansen, Paul W.	P	O-727801	2nd Lt	18	A.C.	"	Unknown	"
N	Josephson, Emanuel J.	N	O-727019	2nd Lt	18	"	"	"	"
R	Galm, Frank J.	R	12087633	Cpl.	38	"	"	Fatal	"
E	Weyrauch, Russell (NMI)	G	16042586	Sgt.	30	"	"	"	"
G	Mengini, James J., Jr.	G	12077706	Cpl.	38	"	"	"	"
X	Nolan, Charles F.	E	32174825	Sgt.	38	"	"	Unknown	"

PILOT CHARGED WITH ACCIDENT

(20) Hodge Grover C. (21) O-789226 (22) 1st Lt. (23) 18 (24) A.C.
(Last name) (First name) (Middle initial) (Serial number) (Rank) (Personnel class) (Branch)

Assigned (25) Air Transport (26) 319th Bomb. (27) 440th Bomb. (28) in transit
(Command and Air Force) (Group) (Squadron) (Station)

Attached for flying (29) (30) (31) (32)
(Command and Air Force) (Group) (Squadron) (Station)

Original rating (33) P (34) 4-29-42 Present rating (35) P (36) 4-29-42 Instrument rating (37) 7-20-42
(Rating) (Date) (Rating) (Date) (Date)

FIRST PILOT HOURS: No record this station
(at the time of this accident)

(38) This type approximately 375:00 (42) Instrument time last 6 months approx. 11:00
(39) This model 300:00 (43) Instrument time last 30 days 1:00
(40) Last 90 days 50:00 (44) Night time last 6 months 100:00
(41) Total 700:00 (45) Night time last 30 days 0:00

AIRCRAFT DAMAGE

	DAMAGE		(49) LIST OF DAMAGED PARTS
(46) Aircraft	M		
(47) Engine(s)	M	M	
(48) Propeller(s)	M	M	

(50) Weather at the time of accident

(51) Was the pilot flying on instruments at the time of accident No
(52) Cleared from Onoto (53) To Alkali (54) Kind of clearance Contact or on top of broken clouds

(55) Pilot's mission Ferrying aircraft to Presque Isle, Me. for rerouting to South Atlantic.

(56) Nature of accident Aircraft forced to land.

(57) Cause of accident Aircraft became lost due to radio equipment becoming inoperative and faulty navigation.

RESTRICTED

167

DESCRIPTION OF ACCIDENT

(Brief narrative of accident. Include statement of responsibility and recommendations for action to prevent repetition)

From the notes left by the pilot, the following is presumed to have happened:

After departing from BW-1, the pilot was forced to go on instruments. After some time he turned to the Southwest till he found a break in the clouds and descended through in order to fly CFR. Navigator gave a correction to get back on the course, but evidently the correction was too large. The pilot tuned in on the Goose Bay range approximately half way between BW-1 and Goose Bay and after receiving the signal for a short space of time, the set evidently went dead.

The pilot attempted to use the radio compass and the liaison set, but failed to receive any signal from the Goose Bay range.

The flight continued on the corrected course given by the Navigator till the East coast of Labrador was reached. At that point the Pilot decided they were South of the course and headed North along the coast line. After some time the Pilot realized they were North of the course and nearly out of fuel, so he turned around and headed South, at the same time looking for a place to land.

They found a spot that looked fairly good for a crash landing so went in with the wheels up. The bomb bay was ripped open and one prop tip went thru the fuselage just in back of the pilot. Evidently there were no injuries to any of the crew members.

The aircraft made a crash landing approximately 20 miles North of Hebron, Labrador, although at that time the crew did not know the approximate position.

Three of the crew members, after a few days, struck out for Goose Bay and were never heard of. The four remaining crew members evidently died of exposure and exhaustion.

RECOMMENDATIONS: None.

WILLIAM R. WALNER
Major, Air Corps

Signature T. L. Boyd

T. L. BOYD, Lt. Colonel, A.C.
A-3, North Atlantic Wing, ATC
Presque Isle, Maine

Date May 15, 1943

JESSE W. HAWS
Captain, Air Corps

THE DIARY OF ONE NOW DEAD

Tom Drodge was born in Little Heart's Ease, Trinity Bay, in 1949 and grew up in Clarenville, where he resides today. He attended Horwood High School and Clarenville District Vocational School and has worked as an industrial electrician. Tom is the author of *Under the Radar: A Newfoundland Disaster.*

Index

Visit Flanker Press at:

www.flankerpress.com

https://www.facebook.com/flankerpress

https://twitter.com/FlankerPress

http://www.youtube.com
/user/FlankerPress